················ MAKING SENSE OF ················
Tongues, Interpretation & Prophecy

When the Spirit Speaks

Warren D. Bullock

FOREWORD BY GEORGE O. WOOD

GPH™

Gospel Publishing House
Springfield, Missouri
02-0467

© 2009 by Gospel Publishing House, 1445 N. Boonville Ave., Springfield,
Missouri 65802. All rights reserved. No part of this book may be reproduced,
stored in a retrieval system, or transmitted in any form or by any means –
electronic, mechanical, photocopy, recording, or otherwise – without prior
written permission of the copyright owner, except for brief quotations used
in connection with reviews in magazines or newspapers.

ISBN 978-0-88243-284-7

Printed in United States of America

Contents

To My Wife and
Partner in Ministry

Judi

Foreword

How can we best encourage the exercise of the vocal gifts of the Spirit in a local church setting?

I faced this question as the pastor of a church that experienced seventeen straight years of growth. The Spirit helped us keep the balance between order and spontaneity.

I taught our congregation that a vocal spiritual gift must meet three criteria:

- It must bring honor to Christ.
- It must edify the believers.
- It must be a positive influence on unbelievers present.

If it failed any of these three tests, then what was expressed was really not in accord with the Scripture.

I strongly believe that Warren Bullock's book will bring great help to pastors and ministers as they build an encouraging atmosphere in congregations for the vocal gifts of the Spirit to be welcomed. There is such sound biblical and pastoral counsel in this book.

As Pentecostal people, let's not settle for an atmosphere in our services where everything is totally programmed. Let's leave room for the spontaneous expressions of vocal spiritual gifts. But, these gifts must be expressed in an excellent way; and the leader of the service must explain them intelligibly to those present who have never been in such an atmosphere.

I trust every pastor will take advantage of this most helpful and balanced work on the vocal spiritual gifts—and that churches will use it in Bible studies, midweek services, and small groups so that the people in our churches will have the benefit of this sound guidance.

George O. Wood
General Superintendent

Introduction

At a pastors' conference, I was wrapping up a teaching session on the gifts of tongues, interpretation of tongues, and prophecy, when an attendee posed this question: "What books do you recommend that would help us pastors with practical guidelines on how vocal gifts function?"

Having read scores of books on the gifts of the Holy Spirit, I should have had an answer, but I didn't. I was hard pressed to think of a single book that I could recommend on the vocal gifts. This lack of resources may be due in part to writers who are cessationist in their perspective—those who believe the gifts of the Spirit (1 Corinthians 12) ended in the first century—and who disavow the necessity of these gifts in the church today. Other authors offer only a cursory overview of the gifts, or else pen weighty theological ruminations about them. Neither approach offers useful helps to pastors like the one asking the sincere and appropriate question at the conference.

Pentecostal and Charismatic authors sometimes take a defensive posture regarding supernatural gifts. It is true that over the years our detractors have put us on the defensive. They have assailed both our doctrine and practices, sometimes with justification. Many non-Pentecostals continue to deny the necessity for supernatural vocal gifts. Some attacks have been done in ignorance, but others have been purposely aggressive and occasionally mean-spirited. Consequently, the Pentecostals' response has been to rise up in defense of valued theological positions, and their arguments and attitudes have some-times matched the harshness of their critics. Certainly a need for a

Pentecostal apologetic exists, but arguments from Spirit-filled writers can become so labored and edgy that one is left to wonder whom the writers are trying to convince—their readers or themselves! And still the pastor is left with no adequate resource to help him or her lead a Pentecostal worship service that welcomes the proper use of vocal gifts.

The goal of this book is to provide simple, clear, practical direction to a pastor and congregation regarding the biblical purpose and function of the three vocal gifts—prophecy, speaking in different kinds of tongues, and the interpretation of tongues (1 Corinthians 12:10). It is not a heavy theological tome, though of necessity it deals with the doctrine of the Holy Spirit—pneumatology. It does not mount a defense against non-Pentecostal viewpoints of these gifts, though a positive presentation of the gifts can be effective in moderating previously negative perspectives. This is not a verse-by-verse commentary of the salient biblical passages regarding these speaking gifts, but it is deeply rooted in Scripture, especially the writings of the apostle Paul.

This is a book for pastors. It seeks to broaden their understanding of the vocal gifts, while offering guidelines for their operation in the worship service. Some ministers have not received adequate teaching on how to encourage, guide, correct, and respond to these gifts. They are willing for God to use them and members of their congregations, but lack know-how in Pentecostal leadership. Because pastors have witnessed misuse and abuse of these gifts, some are cautious, even suspicious, about allowing them to flow freely in church services. Worries abound over alienating unchurched guests. Pastors are rightly concerned about providing adequate safeguards against misuse of the gifts, the maintenance of spiritual balance, and dealing with those motivated by self-interest. But they need assistance with these issues and others, and this book seeks to provide that help.

In addition, pastors can use this little volume as a text when teaching on the vocal gifts. It follows a simple subject-outline that covers the essentials on these three vocal gifts. It answers questions that many people have regarding their use. It even suggests public responses for specific situations that pastors may face in governing these gifts.

This book is for Pentecostal people. The excitement of new believers for their next step in God opens opportunities to share about the Pentecostal experience and the supernatural gifts of the Spirit. Some who have followed the Lord for years may not yet have experienced their own personal Pentecost, but harbor a deep desire for more of the Spirit. Others may have enjoyed their walk with the Spirit for decades, and still maintain the sharp edge of hunger for more of God. The beauty of our relationship with God is that He always

> *God always has more of himself to reveal to us.*

has more of himself to reveal to us. Whatever our level of spiritual maturity, a greater revelation of God always awaits us. And the Spirit is the "Great Revealer" of Christ and the secrets of the Kingdom. God's people are hungry to know more about how the Spirit works through these gifts.

This book is for prospective pastors. I have had the privilege of teaching hundreds of students who are preparing for ministry. I truly love their openness to the Spirit and ready response to His work in their life. They are spongelike in receiving truth. They will challenge, question, argue, and debate, not out of rebellion or spite, but in pursuit of truth. In most cases, Pentecost is their passion. But they want reality, not phony, superspiritual dramatics. They want the Pentecostal gifts to contribute effectively to reaching people who are far from God. It is my hope that this book could provide help to them through use as a text in church-based Bible institutes, Master's Commissions, Bible schools, and Schools of Ministry.

It is my sincere desire that *When the Spirit Speaks: Making Sense of Tongues, Interpretation, and Prophecy* will contribute to the primary purpose for which the vocal gifts are given—the building up of the body of Christ.

1

A Crisis of Confusion

Rediscovering Our Pentecostal Identity

I was invited to speak on the work of the Holy Spirit by a bright young pastor of a relatively new congregation. I have met many young men and women in ministry just like him. Raised in a Pentecostal church, he had experienced his own personal baptism in the Spirit. Praying in tongues was a daily norm. On matters of the Spirit his doctrinal foundations were solid. He held ministerial credentials from a well-known and highly respected Pentecostal fellowship. Reaching lost people was his passion. He was quick to affirm the need of his church for the power of the Spirit.

And yet this new pastor was wrestling with an uneasiness about the manifestations of the Spirit. He had seen abuses, especially with vocal gifts, which had gone uncorrected on the premise that such correction would quench the Spirit. Excesses that claimed the Spirit's authorship had embarrassed him at times. He was in the uncomfortable position of desiring the Spirit's work while also fearing a repeat of fleshly aberrations.

Interestingly, his models for public worship and ministry were not Pentecostal, but were the pastors of some of America's great evangelical megachurches. In those churches you would not find healing lines or vocal gifts or invitations to receive Spirit baptism. And yet as evangelicals, these pastors and their churches are reaching scores of people for Christ.

By contrast, many Pentecostal and Charismatic churches in America are on a growth plateau or are declining[1] even though Pentecostals claim to be identified with spiritual harvest.[2] So this young pastor wonders what advantage being Pentecostal provides. That he could even think in terms of an advantage disturbs him, because it implies a smug superiority he does not feel and suggests an attitude with which he refuses to identify. His negative experience with spiritual gifts has created the mind-set that most spiritual manifestations are obstacles, not helps, to bringing people to Christ. Yet he has experienced too much reality through the Spirit to be comfortable denying His supernatural power.

This pastor has a spiritual identity crisis, and, in my opinion, he represents a generation of young preachers in Pentecostal and Charismatic circles. Is he a Pentecostal or an Evangelical? And will he build a church that is Pentecostal in practice as well as doctrine, or will his church follow the patterns of ministry of the strong evangelical churches he admires?

Private vs. Public

One solution some have used to resolve this Evangelical/ Pentecostal dilemma is to receive the baptism in the Spirit and enjoy the benefits that flow from that blessing, but not publicly promote such spiritual experience. They opt to keep private use of tongues separate from public manifestations of the gifts of tongues and interpretation. They regularly pray in the Spirit as part of their devotional experience, as do many in their congregations. They value the personal edification that praying in tongues provides and acknowledge that proper public uses of the vocal gifts also bless the church. But fear of misuse eventually leads to disuse.

The church's doctrinal statements may include written validation of the vocal gifts. Verbal affirmation of those doctrines may be given so that the congregation is tied firmly to its pneumatological moorings, its belief in the Holy Spirit and super-natural gifts. However, in practice supernatural vocal gifts are rare, and while they are not actively discouraged, neither are they specifically encouraged. In most services, Spirit-led opportunities for vocal gifts are not provided, and when these gifts are absent for prolonged periods, no one seems to miss them. Those who are uninitiated concerning supernatural gifts don't know what they have missed because they have never experienced these gifts.

One is tempted to conclude that this is an issue of worship style. One style of worship would encourage the speaking gifts, but another style would not. There's no denying the variety of styles of worship in churches. The Church of Jesus Christ is incredibly diverse. What a normal worship style is in Nigeria, Africa, might seem strange in Nome, Alaska. Latin styles of worship might seem foreign to Asians. Even worship in the Bible Belt, USA, could be unfamiliar in other parts of the country.

But the vocal gifts and their purposes remain the same. The decision to follow the "private/public" approach is not primarily an issue of worship style.

Believers Only

Other Spirit-filled pastors resolve this Evangelical/Pentecostal tension by affirming that vocal gifts are for believers' services only. So in a prayer meeting or a small group setting, where non-believers are not present, the speaking gifts would be acceptable, even encouraged.[3] But in the public services on Sunday where it is most likely that the unchurched would be present, they would not be allowed.

The rationale for this approach rests primarily on the "sign" passage of 1 Corinthians 14 (verses 20–25), and verse 23 in particular: "So if the whole church comes together and everyone speaks in tongues, and some who do not understand or some unbelievers come in, will they not say that you are out of your mind?" So to avoid the prospect of an unbeliever hearing someone speaking in tongues, this gift is consigned to "believers only" meetings. If we allow these vocal gifts in all worship services, so the argument goes, then visitors unversed in the things of the Spirit will think we are crazy.

Consigning the speaking gifts to believers' only meetings seems to be "throwing the baby out with the bath water." Based on shaky exegesis, the determination is made that no vocal gifts will be received in public services. But what if the sovereign Holy Spirit, who gives the gifts as He determines, prompts a believer to use a vocal gift? What if an unbeliever hears a powerful interpretation to speaking in tongues? Or what if a prophecy is given?

> But if an unbeliever or someone who does not understand comes in while everybody is prophesying, he will be convinced by all that he is a sinner and will be judged by all, and the secrets of his heart will be laid bare. So he will fall down and worship God, exclaiming, 'God is really among you!' (1 Corinthians 14:24,25).

Is this not the kind of response that we pray for? Isn't this part of the desired harvest? But it is not a possibility if the speaking gifts are relegated to believers' services only.

The vocal gifts are designed by the Spirit to work in every community and in every church.

Trying to select the services in which the Holy Spirit will work through vocal gifts confuses sovereignty and strategy. Every church wanting to reach those who are far from God will employ strategies designed for that purpose. That also means that other strategies will not be utilized. Strategic decisions will be made based on the demographics and culture of the community and related factors.

However, vocal gifts are not a strategy about which we can make a positive or negative determination. They are designed by the Spirit to work in every community and in every church to assist in reaching all kinds of people. The sovereignty of the Spirit determines the time and place of their usage. A pastoral meeting for strategic planning is not the place to decide that "As part of our strategy to reach the lost, we will have vocal gifts only in believers' services." That is a contradiction.

> *The Holy Spirit will never sponsor any vocal gift that will drive people away from Christ.*

It seems evident that Paul preferred prophecy to tongues and interpretation. He decried the frequent Corinthian practice of speaking in tongues publicly without interpretation. Nevertheless he encouraged both prophecy and interpreted tongues in all services. His was not a decision based on developing a strategy, but on his understanding of the Spirit's work and power. He did not talk about two different and separate services one for believers in which vocal gifts were permissible, and one for believers and non-believers where they were not. His is a unified approach, but with an important emphasis on the need for tongues to be interpreted.

Pastors who arbitrarily decide where and when vocal gifts will be allowed do so without firm biblical basis. This is not to deny the need for strong pastoral leadership. But we must be cautious about making decisions that not only are not Spirit-led, but are in conflict with what the Spirit is trying to accomplish. The bottom line for the pastor, the church, and the Spirit is people finding Christ. The Holy Spirit will never sponsor any vocal gift that will drive people away from Christ.

Both/And

What if these conflicted, Spirit-filled pastors did not argue either in favor of the successful Evangelical models or against their roots in Pentecostal theology? What if they acknowledged that positive models and deep roots are both important? What if they preserved the evan-

> *The positive benefits of balance in worship are inestimable.*

gelistic fervor of the much-admired megachurches while acknowledging that the Holy Spirit and His gifts would never stifle that fervor? What if they accepted that to be Evangelical they did not have to be anti-Pentecostal? What if they resolved their pastoral identity crisis by recognizing that they are both Evangelical and Pentecostal? Rather than fall into the either/or trap, what if they embraced the reality of both/and?

Okay, let's say that they did. So what? As it relates to the vocal gifts, what difference would it make? In addition to accepting the bedrock doctrines of evangelicalism, they would also have to take seriously the double imperatives given by the apostle Paul: "Do not forbid speaking in tongues" (1 Corinthians 14:39), and "Do not treat prophecies with contempt" (1 Thessalonians 5:20). These verses do not provide much wiggle room for the "private vs. public" pastor, or the "believers only" pastor. These imperatives do not suggest a variety of styles, strategies, or options to be considered. The most extensive biblical treatment of vocal gifts—1 Corinthians 14—assumes that those gifts, along with others, will be a normal part of corporate worship. They will not overbalance other aspects of worship in the way the Corinthian church was overemphasizing tongues. But neither will other forms of worship be so overbalanced that these gifts are excluded. The positive benefits of such balance in worship are inestimable.

But we must also ask what difference it will make if Spirit-filled pastors don't buy into the both/and perspective. What if Pentecostal pastors withdraw from their roots to embrace an evangelicalism that ignores Paul's double imperative? What happens to the pastor and the Spirit-filled church that forbid speaking in tongues and hold prophecy in contempt by disallowing it? Is the pastor indeed violating the Scripture and if so, what will be the result of that disobedience? What negative dynamics are released when reaching the seeker pushes the pastor to take a non- or anti-Pentecostal stance? What will happen to the church that fails to receive the positive benefits of the vocal gifts due to the pastor's decision to forbid them?

For the Church

What will happen? In some cases, believe it or not, the church will thrive. Where the pastor has a true fervor to reach those far from God and develops strategies to reach them, people will indeed find Christ and the church will grow. The pastor's passion, whether recognized or not, comes from the Spirit. So to the degree the pastor flows with the Spirit, God will build the church. Unfortunately the church's growth will then be used to validate the conviction that God doesn't really care about spiritual gifts as long as people are being reached. And of course, the argument will be made that nothing is more Pentecostal than bringing people to Christ.

> *If I know the good that vocal gifts can do and deny my congregation those benefits, I stand responsible.*

Despite the Pentecostal doctrinal statement of the church or its denomination, this growing church has moved sharply away from its roots. The supernatural gifts, including the vocal gifts, have been driven underground. Since those new to the faith know nothing about this dimension of the Spirit's work, they have no hunger for it, nor do they sense any pain by its absence. Veterans of Pentecost rejoice at those finding Christ and supplement their personal growth through their private prayer language.

However, not all churches will thrive. Some will slowly die. Where the pastor's passion for the lost is not primary, then withdrawal from all things Pentecostal isn't going to help reach seekers. When adopting a non-Pentecostal stance is a pragmatic decision and seeks simply to imitate what others do without any alternative strategies, it is self-defeating.

So some Pentecostal-turned-Evangelical churches thrive and some die. But isn't that also true for those that are fervently Pentecostal? Of course. So what difference does it make if you are Evangelical or Pentecostal? Just this.

Every person will be judged on the basis of the truth they know and understand (Romans 2:2). If I comprehend the value God places on the supernatural gifts and know the double imperatives He has issued, I will be judged for that knowledge and my response to it. If I know the good that vocal gifts can do and deny my congregation those benefits, I stand responsible. If I ignore not only the Word, but the urgings of the Spirit regarding vocal gifts, I will have to answer for my disobedience to the Scripture and my sleight of the Holy Spirit. If my church did not develop because of my spiritual drift, I will be held accountable.

If great Evangelical and Pentecostal churches are both being developed and if I have received understanding about spiritual manifestations, why not build a great Pentecostal church in harmony with Evangelical principles? Why not embrace both/and? Instead of following other models, why not become the model that other churches could follow? Why not let passion for those far from God be fueled by Pentecostal worship, including gift ministries? Why not receive the powerful benefits of the vocal gifts? Why not?

For the Pastor

What will happen to the pastors who take a path away from their Pentecostal home? If their church succeeds, they will rejoice. But on a personal level, they may suffer for knowing the truth, but not doing it. When we are not true to ourselves, the external trappings of achievement wear thin. Inner conflict over biblical values can cause frustration, even depression. The yearning for "something more" is ever present, driving the pastor toward God. In turn, there is a longing that the church know that deeper experience too. The pastor may resolve this internal crisis by withdrawing from his Pentecostal fellowship. But he cannot withdraw from what he knows of the Spirit.

If the church does not do well, then the pastor may begin to doubt himself and his calling. Yet if he is true to what he believes, he can continue to walk in integrity.

How is it possible for the local church to keep the balance between solid evangelicalism and biblical Pentecostalism? How can a church maintain its spiritual balance and identity? The answer to this question is simple—the pastor. God in His goodness provided a shepherd who would lead the flock into possession of its spiritual identity in Christ.

Endnotes

[1] Admittedly, this is a broad generalization. Certainly, there are many vibrant growing Pentecostal and Charismatic churches. The reader is encouraged to do his or her own statistical analysis regarding churches in plateau and decline.

[2] The initial outpouring of the Holy Spirit came during the Jewish Feast of Pentecost, a celebration of the harvest.

[3] When the author specifically asked pastors whether the vocal gifts are active in small groups settings, not once has the answer been yes.

2

Shepherds on the Spot

Three Guiding Principles for Pastors

Some pastoral lessons are only learned in the school of the Spirit. Blessed is the pastor who learns about the Spirit's work through godly mentors, personal Bible study, keen observation, Bible school classes, or on-the-job training. All contribute positively to the pastor's spiritual growth and understanding, but none can substitute for a consistent day-to-day walk in the Spirit. We learn best about the Spirit's ways by interaction with the Spirit himself. We can read about His power, but only by experiencing that power do we begin to understand it. True, experience not rooted in sound doctrine can push the fringes of fanaticism. But doctrine devoid of experience will never be lifechanging. The blending of theology with experience produces a pastoral ministry that is grounded in the unchanging Word, yet still enjoys the creative, dynamic leadership of the Spirit.

At age twenty-six, I stepped into my first senior pastor position. My congregation consisted of sixteen adults, nearly all of them older than I. Though I had been raised in church, I was not nearly as mature in the faith as these dear saints. But in the process of pastoring, I grew with the church. I made my share of mistakes, but the congregation allowed for them. They forgave my ill-advised initiatives. Some even offered gentle correction. They understood that I was a novice, but they nurtured me through prayer and understanding. As a result, I continued to develop in my spiritual perceptions and awareness.

My father had been the best example that I had known of how to pastor a Spirit-filled church. Growing up, I watched what he did and how he did it. I had no intention of going into ministry, but when God directed that way and I became a first-time pastor, I soon learned that watching was not the same as doing. My father's comfortable and stable relationship with the

> *Following the voice of the Spirit is a skill that is honed through both prayer and error.*

Spirit made his leadership look easy, but when I assumed the pastor's role, I discovered that following the voice of the Spirit is a skill that is honed through both prayer and error. Prayer increases one's sensitivities to the Spirit, and error helps you know when you missed His direction. You learn and grow from both.

Today's church congregations in general have a much higher expectation level for their leaders than when I began pastoring. Young men and women are expected to possess extraordinary gifts, produce consistent numerical growth, and exercise mature leadership even though they are first-time pastors. Errors are seldom tolerated. When these young leaders make mistakes, as they inevitably will, criticism may come their way rather than encouragement. Instead of support and nurture, they and their families may be disparaged. While there certainly are exceptions, churches usually expect first-time pastors to have graduate degrees in the school of the Spirit. They are rarely given the opportunity to grow with their church.

This is unfortunate for both the church and the pastor. The church suffers because it reaps the bad fruit of criticism—conflict, contests over control, and accelerated pastoral turnover. The positive mission the church is supposed to advance is subverted by its negative response to leadership. The pastor suffers through lack of support and love, and is battered by constant challenges to visionary thinking. This hostile environment does little to foster personal spiritual development. Ultimately, he or she may question his or her calling, or leave ministry because of the emotional toll inflicted on them and their families.

Congregations have a right to expect solid, if not spectacular, Spirit-directed leadership from their pastor. It is not an unreasonable expectation that a pastor live with integrity, in harmony with the Word, and in tune with the Spirit. But neither congregational members nor pastors live without error. Rather than carp and criticize when mistakes are made, would not the church be better strengthened if both the members and the pastor helped one another through forgiveness, encouragement, and correction?

Pastors cannot lead their congregation where they have never been. They will be poor instructors in the things of the Spirit if they do not personally experience the blessings of the Spirit-filled life.[1] They must learn to pray their way into the Spirit's realm and expand their understanding of His purposes and power. Some pastors actually avoid the subject of the Holy Spirit. As one pastor told me, "I don't understand it." Even though he led a church that espoused Pentecostal doctrine, he never taught or preached about the Holy Spirit. Consequently, the church had little understanding about the work of the Spirit and rarely had any supernatural manifestation of the gifts.

If pastors want to lead Spirit-filled fellowships that encourage the vocal gifts, several biblical guidelines may be helpful.

Provide Teaching

Jesus' communication skills were unsurpassed. He spoke with unquestioned authority. He never missed an opportunity to instruct His disciples about the kingdom of God. We look to Him as our prime example of what an anointed preacher/teacher should be like. And the Master Teacher taught about the Holy Spirit. His discourse in John 14–16 provided His disciples and us some of the most valuable and extensive teaching on the person and work of the Spirit that is found in the New Testament.

Jesus understood that the role of the Spirit was changing. In centuries past, the Spirit was a powerful, but hidden, force. His work came primarily through selected individuals who were anointed for specific purposes. But soon that work would be unleashed through the

The biblical response to misuse is not disuse, but correction.

Church as the enduement of the Spirit was made available to every believer in the body of Christ. Jesus' teaching anticipated the outpouring of the Spirit at Pentecost and prepared His disciples for it.

Today's pastor/teacher is privileged to follow Jesus' example and teach about the third Person of the Trinity—the Holy Spirit. New converts, who are born again by the Spirit, need to know that other dynamic works of the Spirit are still awaiting them, not the least of which is the baptism in the Holy Spirit as described in Acts 2:4. Spirit-filled believers need encouragement to enter into the gift ministry, including the vocal gifts, as God provides the enablement. The body of Christ needs to be challenged to renewal and revival that keep fresh our experience in the Spirit. The pastor can meet these needs through consistent teaching and preaching on the Holy Spirit.

The old maxim is true, "You get what you preach for." If you want to encourage Spirit baptism, then you must teach about it. If supernatural manifestations are desired, then faith must be raised in the Spirit's ability to perform signs and wonders. If the church is to receive the benefit of the vocal gifts, then the people must be taught how to be used of God in this way.

Regarding vocal gifts, consider these positive outcomes, some for believers and others for unbelievers, as delineated in 1 Corinthian 14:

- We speak to God and utter mysteries with our spirits (verse 2).
- We are strengthened (verses 3,26).
- We are encouraged (verses 3,31).
- We are comforted (verse 3).
- We are edified and built up (verses 4,12).
- We pray and sing with our spirits (verse 15).
- We praise God with our spirits and give thanks (verse 16).
- The unbeliever is convinced that he is a sinner (verse 24).
- The secrets of the unbeliever's heart are laid bare, and he falls down and worships God (verse 25).
- We receive revelation (verse 30).
- We are instructed (verse 31).

Why would any pastor not want these vibrant, positive results in the congregation he leads? We can have them, but we must teach our people how to correctly and appropriately utilize the vocal gifts. Failure here means that we will deny our people these spiritual outcomes. For their sake, we cannot afford to fail.

Offer Correction

The gifts of tongues, interpretation of tongues, and prophecy can be badly misused. The abuse of these gifts by both well-meaning people and charlatans has brought them into disrepute in some circles. If a continuing cycle of misuse is allowed to continue, then a commensurate negative reaction can be expected. Pastors may respond by simply refusing to allow the vocal gifts to function. The conclusion could be drawn that these gifts are doing more harm than good, so we won't have any of them.

However, the biblical response to misuse is not disuse, but correction. The Corinthian church was clearly misusing the vocal gifts, especially the gift of tongues. But Paul did not recommend that speaking in tongues be suspended. In fact, he urged them not to prohibit speaking in tongues (1 Corinthians 14:39). He also offered both teaching and correction—teaching on how to function in these gifts and correction in regard to their unhealthy practices. Vocal gifts are sometimes misused, not because those who are speaking are bad people

> *Most of God's people welcome the pastor's intervention.*

with deviant motives, but because they don't know any better. That is why God gave pastors to the church—to provide the instruction and correction that will help people flow with the Spirit in harmony with the Word.

So, why are some pastors reluctant to bring needed correction? In my opinion, aversion to bringing correction has one primary source: fear. That fear may come in various forms:

Fear of quenching the Spirit. We are so hungry for moves of God's Spirit that we sometimes tolerate practices that we should not allow. We do not want to infringe on what the Spirit may be doing, especially if we have not seen a manifestation evidenced before in a particular way. There are times when we so yearn for supernatural works that we ignore the checks of the Spirit that warn us when something is not right. If we don't immediately correct aberrations, they become easier to accept when they reoccur.

Fear of failure. Maybe we are inexperienced and afraid of saying the wrong thing. We know correction is needed, but our understanding of the Spirit's operations is limited, and we fear giving the wrong correction. Perhaps our attempts to correct will not be clear. All in all, we may fail and look bad in the process. So to preserve our own image, we don't bring needed correction.

Fear of people. Spirit-filled people long for the supernatural. They so relish manifestations of the Spirit's power that they may view their pastor as an inhibitor of the Spirit's moving because he is a stickler for adhering to biblical guidelines. If correction is offered, this only adds to their perception that the Spirit is being quenched, though that is far from the pastor's intent. Correction then may elicit criticism. Criticism can turn into ongoing opposition. Opposition can develop into hostility, and the "fight or flight" syndrome develops. Some stay to fight, and others take flight from the church. Fear of such a scenario can freeze the pastor's impulse toward correction.

But the pastor should not anticipate that correction will automatically create a negative response. Most of God's people welcome the pastor's intervention because they themselves recognize when a vocal gift is being used improperly. People who have been in Pentecostal churches for any length of time have seen and heard enough quirky vocal gifts to make them appreciate the pastor's initiative not to allow their misuse.

Our first responsibility is to Him, and then to His church.

If a pastor discerns that fear is keeping him from providing needed correction, he should pray for a new understanding of the fear of the Lord—that holy and awesome sense of who God is. The fear of the Lord helps us comprehend more clearly our relationship and responsibility to Him, which in turn motivates us to do the right thing in spite of our fears.

Of the Early Church the Scripture says, "It was strengthened; and encouraged by the Holy Spirit, it grew in numbers, living in the fear of the Lord" (Acts 9:31). Strengthening and encouraging are two of the benefits of the vocal gifts (1 Corinthians 14:3). But we dare not overlook the importance of living in the fear of the Lord. Our first responsibility is to Him, and then to His church.

Knowing that, we can overcome our fears, offer correction with love and grace, and the church will be strengthened and encouraged. More will be said in a later chapter regarding the how-to of correction.

Guard the Flock

Among the exhortations Paul gave the Ephesian elders were these cautions: "Keep watch over . . . all the flock. . . . Be on your guard!" (Acts 20:28,31). He then warned them that wolves would come in among them, even from their own congregation. Their purpose? To distort the truth and draw people away from the church body (Acts 20:29,30). Because the enemy uses similar tactics today, the pastor must aggressively guard the flock.

Misuse of the vocal gifts can be dealt with through teaching and correction. But the motives of those using vocal gifts are harder to test. It would be harder still to prove from Scripture that God never

The Spirit is faithful to provide the insights we need.

uses those who have impure motives! However, a person's character and gifting usually can only be evaluated over time. Such a long-term evaluation can test motives for purity. But even when an on-the-spot, immediate judgment must be made, the Spirit is faithful to provide the insights we need.

Megachurch pastors in metropolitan areas confront unusual challenges in guarding the flock. They cannot possibly know everyone who comes to their church services. So for the spiritual safety of their congregation, they cannot allow an open forum for anyone and everyone to utilize the vocal gifts. That's why some require that the leadership screen vocal gifts before they can be given.

One large church in Seattle includes an announcement in its Sunday bulletin to the effect that while the vocal gifts are welcomed and encouraged, only members of the local congregation may be utilized. In addition, elders are strategically seated throughout the large auditorium, and members must go to an elder for clearance of their vocal gift. The elder then alerts the pastor that a member has a vocal gift, and the pastor determines at what point in the service it will be given. A microphone is provided so that everyone will

The gift is for the church; the church is not for the gift.

be able to hear the vocal gift clearly. As you might expect, it is rare that the pastor ever has to offer correction because a gift has been abused.

We might conclude that this approach lacks spontaneity or is too controlling or gives the pastor too much authority. But the truth is that this pastor has found a way to encourage the vocal gifts while at the same time guarding his congregation from those who are unscrupulous, uninformed, or emotionally distraught.

The church I pastored in Tacoma, Washington, had just completed a major building project, including relocation to a new site. The second Sunday in our new facility, a gentleman whom I did not know gave a vocal gift of tongues, and a member of our congregation gave the interpretation. And yet when this man began speaking in tongues, the Holy Spirit immediately waved a red flag in my spirit. It was as if I were being put on alert, and that I should be on guard against this gentleman even though the vocal gift did not seem to be out of order.

The next Sunday he was back, and he again exercised the gift of tongues, but this time no interpretation followed. So I offered the instruction that the person speaking in tongues publicly should pray for the interpretation. I did not ask him to give the interpretation, but did imply that his vocal gift may have been out of order. He never came back again. I am convinced that he came to our new church to test what would be allowed.

He saw the church only as the place where he could utilize his gift. Such people view the church as a means to an end, the end being the exercise of their particular gift. Shepherds must guard their flock against those who advocate such a perspective. Gifts, including the vocal gifts, are not the end, but the means to the end. Paul said, "The manifestation of the Spirit is given for the common good" (1 Corinthians 12:7).The gift is for the church; the church is not for the gift. So be on your guard!

Pastors have an awesome responsibility summed up in the words: "They keep watch over you as men who must give an account" (Hebrews 13:17). When it comes to the things of the Spirit, they can fulfill that responsibility in part by the consistent teaching of the Word, gentle correction, and fearless protection of the flock.

Endnote

[1] An excellent resource is *Living the Spirit Formed Life* by Jack Hayford (Ventura, CA: Regal Books, 2001).

3
Order in the Church
Three Guiding Principles for Congregations

When studying Scripture, it is helpful to examine what isn't said as well as what is. The main points that an author may lay out have to be given primary focus, but don't miss what could have been said, but wasn't. That can be instructive too.

When the body of Christ wants to know about vocal gifts, it gives attention to the most significant passage on the subject—the fourteenth chapter of 1 Corinthians. But that chapter doesn't say nearly as much as we might think it should, or hope it would. It leaves unanswered questions that we wish it had spoken about. It leaves much unsaid.

For instance, it doesn't say anything about who is qualified to give a vocal gift. And why doesn't it tell us more about the relationship of tongues and interpretation to prophecy? That would have been helpful. Why is the "sign" passage so confounding? Since we are told to judge prophecy, why isn't an objective grid provided by which we could make that judgment? Paul corrected the misuse of the gifts, but did not inform the pastor as to how such correction should be done in real time. Why isn't there more detail about singing in the Spirit? And how would Paul handle misguided and wrongly motivated people who want to be used in vocal gifts? These are questions, among others, that I have asked myself many times.

However, Paul, inspired by the Holy Spirit, is communicating even when he is not answering all the questions we might have. First, by not saying anything about them, he is reminding us that the questions we might have are less important that we think. They are not unimportant, but pale in comparison to what he stated very clearly. Second, what we view as gaps in teaching may allow for flexibility and adaptation in different cultures and in specific circumstances. What is not dealt with could be left to the discretion of the Pentecostal leader to act in keeping with other principles of the Word and the "present tense" guidance of the Spirit. Third, the principles he does set forth are foundational and will apply in every situation, culture, and circumstance. Because the Scripture is our authoritative rule for faith and conduct, the guidelines for the church that are unmistakably set forth are inviolable. Those guidelines are edification, intelligibility, and order.

Edification

Verse 12 is the key to this principle. "Since you are eager to have spiritual gifts, try to excel in gifts that build up the church." So which vocal gifts do or do not edify, or build up? Here's what we can derive from chapter 14.

- Prophecy edifies the church (verse 4).
- Tongues accompanied by interpretation build up the church (verse 5).
- Tongues without an interpretation do not edify the church (verses 16,17).
- Personal prayer languages build up the speaker but do not edify the church (verse 4).

The gift of prophecy builds up, but also strengthens, encourages, comforts, convinces the sinner, reveals, and instructs. It has an immense capacity for helping the church. When interwoven with the preached Word, it lends a spiritual impetus to preaching that is unsurpassed.

Intelligibility

Closely tied to the edification of the church is the issue of intelligibility, which simply means that the church cannot be built up if it doesn't understand what is said. Specifically, tongues without an interpretation create multiple problems, the most significant being that tongues are not understandable. Consequently, the church is left without benefit. Paul illustrated this in three ways.

First, he spoke of lifeless instruments like the flute or harp that have no value unless distinct sounds are put together to form a tune. Second, a trumpet that does not give clear call when it is time to go to battle can create confusion among the soldiers. Third, all the languages of the world have meaning to someone, but not to foreigners. So Paul concluded, "So it is with you. Unless you speak intelligible words

The church cannot be built up if it doesn't understand what is said.

with your tongue, how will anyone know what you are saying? You will just be speaking into the air" (verse 9).

If that is the effect on fellow believers, think of the impact on unbelievers with unintelligible vocal gifts, i.e., tongues without interpretation. They will conclude that we are out of our minds. This is why a clear directive is given that if no interpreter is present, the one who speaks in tongues should keep silent or pray that he might receive the interpretation (verses 13,28). Paul summed up his personal response this way: "But in the church I would rather speak five intelligible words to instruct others than ten thousand words in a tongue" (verse 19).

So why are we still dealing with uninterpreted tongues in our services? Why does this continue to be a problem? On occasion, we still have people speaking in tongues publicly, but no interpretations

are given, a violation of these biblical "edification and intelligibility"
guidelines. Why?

In some cases, the tongues
speakers miss God. They think
the Spirit is prompting them to
speak when He isn't. Or they mis-
take praying in the Spirit, which
is between them and God, for the
gift of tongues designed for the

*Interpretation
and prophecy
require a
blending of the
person's mind
with the mind of
the Spirit.*

whole church. Their exuberance may overflow in an outburst of
tongues that has no relevance to anyone but them. And frankly,
it is much easier to give a message in tongues than to give an
interpretation or prophecy. When we speak in tongues, our minds
are unfruitful; we are praying with our spirits (1 Corinthians
14:14). And tongues cannot be judged because they are unintelligible, whereas interpretation and prophecy require a blending
of the person's mind with the mind of the Spirit. Both of these
intelligible vocal gifts are to be judged which puts the speaker's
credibility on the line.

In other instances, the tongues speaker forges ahead without
knowing whether an interpreter is present. That prompts the question
as to how one knows whether someone is present whom the Spirit
uses to interpret tongues. If you are a guest in a church and are unfamiliar with the congregants, then you can't know if an interpreter is
present. So it is best to remain silent. But if you are in your home
church, you are usually aware of those whom God may use to interpret tongues.

Even then, tongues sometimes go uninterpreted because those
who normally interpret do not do so. Perhaps they are wrestling with
unresolved issues or are overcome by family problems or are not as
sensitive to the Lord as usual. Maybe God wants to use someone else,
and that person is not responsive.

But in all these cases, the Scripture provides a backup, so that the tongues will not go without interpretation. That backup is the tongues speaker. "Anyone who speaks in a tongue should pray that he may interpret what he says" (1 Corinthians 14:13). We will deal with this more in chapter 5, but the obvious conclusion is that God will answer that prayer. The tongues speaker will then give the interpretation, and the church will understand it and be edified.

What about situations where a believer may speak in tongues loudly during praise and worship, but does not intend it to be interpreted? Is it wrong for them to use their prayer language (not the gift of tongues) in a corporate setting with such volume that others can clearly hear them?

Though I have seen and heard this in several instances, it especially came to my attention when I was guest speaker at a small rural church. I thoroughly enjoyed the spirit of the service and the response of the people to the Lord in worship. I had a keen appreciation for the fine pastor. The auditorium was not large, nor was the congregation, but spiritual life was evident. During the worship and praise, one lady began to pray in the Spirit rather loudly. This was not a single outburst, but a strong, sustained time of prayer in tongues, even during the singing. When there would be a break in the singing or a pause in the service, you could hear her speaking in tongues. I sat there wondering if there were any unbelievers present. But even as a believer, I was not edified.

In my opinion, this illustrates a misuse of tongues, and violates the principles of edification and intelligibility. Who was able to understand this lady? Who was built up by her praise in tongues? No one. She should have prayed quietly in the Spirit to herself.

What about those church settings where everyone is encouraged to pray in the Spirit and a massive volume of tongues is released? These can be times of refreshing and power, but must nevertheless bow to the guidelines of Scripture. Such corporate tongues should be released when only believers are present. These tongues will have no interpretation. If an unbeliever is present, the tongues will be unintelligible and consequently not helpful. In fact, such corporate tongues speaking will tend to have a negative effect, rather than positive.

Some of the worst offenders on this point are ministers. How often have you heard the pastor pray in the Spirit using a microphone? Everybody hears the tongues, but no one understands it. In my opinion, the pastor should refrain from praying in tongues unless he or she is prepared to interpret what is said.

Ministers of the gospel should not use their pulpits to do what they will not allow their people to do.

I have cringed while watching Christian television as the preachers speak in tongues all over "television land." For what purpose? Their own edification. No one else is edified, because no one else has a clue what is being said. Ministers of the gospel should not use their pulpits to do what they will not allow their people to do. Ministers should be the first to align themselves with the mandates of the Word that require tongues to be interpreted in public services, or else they should keep silent.

From another perspective, some vocal gifts are not understandable because no microphones are used, and consequently no one can hear. This does not speak to the validity of a vocal gift, but merely points out that unless people can hear a vocal gift clearly, they cannot understand it, and therefore cannot be edified by it.

Order

This third guideline for the church is summed up in two verses in 1 Corinthians 14. Verse 33 reminds us, "God is not a God of disorder but of peace." And Paul concludes the chapter by saying, "But everything should be done in a fitting and orderly way" (verse 40).

The whole chapter serves to illustrate this principle of order in the use of the vocal gifts. One can't read it without the sense that the vocal gifts are inherently free and spontaneous. They are not the result of previous study or forethought. The Spirit prompts unrehearsed speech, both known and unknown. He may use people that we would not. The process of releasing vocal gifts in a public service is largely uncontrived.

But spontaneity should not foster disorder. There is a Spirit-led order, a "fitting and orderly way" (verse 40), when each speaker follows the guidelines of the Word, is sensitive to the Spirit's voice, and is faithful to deliver God's message in a wholly spontaneous way.

Spontaneity should not foster disorder.

Failure to maintain order violates God's character, because He is not a God of disorder.

While we might wish for more detail in how the vocal gifts are to function, we can be satisfied that if we follow the principles of edification, intelligibility, and order, our churches will receive the benefit.

4

Everyday People and Supernatural Language

Who Should Use Vocal Gifts?

If a *Who's Who in Israel* had been published in Jesus' day, you would have searched in vain for the names of the twelve disciples (Matthew 10:2–4). Their personal deficiencies, character flaws, and lack of success would have disqualified them from any ecclesiastical recognition. Yet, Jesus chose such men to become the foundation stones of His Church (Ephesians 2:20). In fact, He continues to call and use unlikely people, choosing "the foolish things of the world to shame the wise," and "the weak things of the world to shame the strong" (1 Corinthians 1:27). He chooses "the lowly things of this world and the despised things—and the things that are not—to nullify the things that are, so that no one may boast before him" (verses 28,29).

It is amazing that God would choose to use any of us to accomplish His purposes! Yet, He does. His enablements now allow us to accomplish what our weaknesses would normally keep us from achieving. How? By the power of the Spirit. The Holy Spirit in His people and the gifts He distributes among them are the tools God uses to accomplish His holy intentions on earth.

So what about the vocal gifts? Whom will God use to deliver a supernatural word to the church?

The Many or the Few

Toward the end of a list of rhetorical questions on spiritual gifts, the apostle Paul asked, "Do all speak in tongues? Do all interpret?" (1 Corinthians 12:30). The implied answer is, "No, not all of God's people will speak with tongues or interpret." More specifically, not everyone will exercise these gifts in a public worship service. But that limitation has nothing to do with the deficiencies of the individual, but rather with God's purposes for that particular congregation. All Spirit-baptized people could use vocal gifts, but not all will. The potential for all of the supernatural gifts is resident within the believer, because the Holy Spirit lives there. But since He gives the gifts "to each one, just as he determines" (1 Corinthians 12:11), He will not release vocal gifts to everyone attending a public service.

The Novice or the Mature

So to whom will He give vocal gifts? We don't know. That is His choice. However, we do know that those who use supernatural vocal gifts are not more spiritual, more holy, or more mature than anyone else. The fact that God may use a particular person to give a prophecy is not a sign that he or she has reached a higher level of spiritual maturity than anyone else. That becomes obvious when prophecies flow through those who have only recently been converted. Their maturity levels are at the "crawling stage." We might expect that God would not use someone so immature in the faith, but He does.

If we think that our spirituality helps us earn God's gifts, then we are saying that they do not flow from grace, but are a reward for our works. That attitude was a core issue in the church at Corinth. Those who were used in gift ministries, especially those who spoke in tongues publicly, viewed themselves as more spiritual than others; they felt that they were at a higher level of spirituality than those around them. But that assertion violated the basic meaning of the gifts (Gk., *charismata*), which are rooted in grace (Gk., *charis*). Gifts of grace are given, not because of merit, but because of God's goodness to His people.

My father helped me understand this principle by giving me a weekly allowance with no strings attached. Because I wanted a higher allowance, I persistently tried to link it to the chores that I was required to do. My thinking was that the more chores I did, the more allowance money Dad would give me. Not so. From Dad's perspective I did my chores as a responsible, contributing member of the Bullock family, and not because I got paid to do them. The chores would be done whether I got an allowance or not! So what I received then in weekly allowance was a gift, free and clear of any obligations, not wages for duties completed.

Spiritual gifts derive from God's grace, and are not the product of our effort.

Gifts are given; wages are earned. Spiritual gifts derive from God's grace, and are not the product of our effort or payoff for years of service. The surprise is that God chooses to allow the gifts to operate through us. We certainly haven't done anything to deserve that privilege.

Saved or Spirit Baptized

Those who "eagerly desire spiritual gifts" (1 Corinthians 14:1) often ask whether it is necessary to be baptized in the Holy Spirit with the evidence of speaking in tongues before the supernatural gifts (outlined in 1 Corinthians 12:8-10) can operate through them. Is Spirit baptism required prior to being used in the supernatural gift ministry? Is Spirit baptism a mandatory entry-level experience after which these gifts can then function? To be even more focused: Can the vocal gifts—tongues, the interpretation of tongues, and prophecy—be spoken by someone who is not Spirit baptized?

In order to adequately answer that question, we must separate the gift of tongues from its interpretation and from prophecy. When we look just at the gift of tongues, the answer as to whom God will use through this gift then rests on two assumptions.

First, we assume that the Pentecostal experience includes speaking in tongues. When the 120 believers in Acts 2 were "baptized with the Holy Spirit" (Acts 1:5), or were "filled with the Holy Spirit," they "began to speak in other tongues as the Spirit enabled them" (Acts 2:4). Not all would agree that speaking in tongues is required to be Spirit baptized, but all must agree that is what occurred at Pentecost. The Spirit provides an unlimited variety of supernatural experiences for the believer to enjoy, but a Pentecostal experience as described in Acts 2:4 will include speaking with tongues.

The second assumption is based on the first. The person who has not received the baptism in the Spirit with the evidence of speaking in tongues will not be used through the gift of tongues in a worship service. Personal Spirit baptism must precede the public gift of tongues. The former is the doorway to the latter.

But can an interpretation of tongues or a prophecy be given by a believer who is not Spirit baptized according the Acts 2:4? The short and simple answer is, "Yes." Note these responses from 1 Corinthians 12:

- The Spirit gives His gifts "to each one, just as he determines" (verse 11).
- "To each one the manifestation of the Spirit is given for the common good" (verse 7).
- "You are the body of Christ, and each one of you is a part of it" (verse 27).

This biblical emphasis on each one underscores the universality of the gifts and their wide distribution by the Spirit to the church. Verses 12 through 26 emphasize the importance of each member and their function in the body. Paul assumed that all the Corinthians were Spirit baptized. Nevertheless, membership in the Body and exercising gifts within it is seen as the result of being "baptized by one Spirit into one body" (verse 13), i.e., salvation. As a member of the body of Christ through salvation, every believer may be used of the Spirit and His gifts to operate within the Body for its strengthening and encouragement.

So those who have not been Spirit baptized according to Acts 2:4 will not speak in tongues for interpretation, but could give interpretations of tongues or prophecies. However, in practice it is rare for non-Pentecostals to be used in this way. Some take an antisupernatural stance toward these gifts. Others contend for the cessation of the gifts, including the vocal gifts. Still others are convinced that since we now have the Bible, vocal gifts are unnecessary. But whatever the reasoning, non-Pentecostals do not seem to anticipate the supernatural works of God with the same fervor as Pentecostals and Charismatics. It isn't that God wouldn't use them in supernatural ways, but it doesn't seem to occur to them that He would want to. Consequently the preponderance of vocal gifts comes from Spirit baptized Pentecostal or Charismatic believers.

The Message or the Messenger

Because God is willing to use any believer, He sometimes speaks through unlikely messengers, even some we don't like! The Old Testament prophets were not always the most popular people in town. Ahab, king of Israel, summed up his feeling about the prophet, Micaiah, when he said, "I hate him because he never prophesies anything good about me, but always bad" (1 Kings 22:8). We are not usually that vehement in our feelings about those God chooses to use, but we sometimes wish He had selected someone else to be His spokesperson. Therefore, we may fail to hear God's message because we don't like the messenger.

Follow this imaginary scenario. Brother Freeman gave a prophecy last Sunday. The congregation responded positively to it. Even though you couldn't find fault with anything he said, you know about some of Brother Freeman's character flaws. You have observed the harshness with which he treats his wife and children. You have heard the sharpness of his criticism of others. And when you went through a recent hardship, he certainly was less than compassionate. Because you know him so well, you cannot receive the word from the Lord he gives. The impact

The gifts are given at His discretion, not yours or mine.

of the prophecy is lost, because you don't like the flawed person God selected to deliver it.

God has a real problem. He has no perfect Christians to use. His "worker pool" is stuffed with the flawed, the inadequate, the inconsistent, the smart but unwise, and those who are zealous but lack knowledge. He would always like to find an Isaiah, but sometimes He must make do with a Balaam.

God has a second problem—you and me. Does He really have to get our permission before using someone of whom we disapprove of? Of course not, but our attitudes reflect that we wish He would at least consult us first so we could give Him the benefit of our wise counsel.

God ignores both problems, and chooses whom He wills. The gifts are given at His discretion, not yours or mine. Our response must be to hear God's clear message, even when He may select an unlikely candidate to deliver it.

The Willing and the Obedient

Have you ever considered that God might want to use you in a vocal gift of tongues, interpretation of tongues, or prophecy? The question is not whether He will use you, but whether you are willing for Him to do so. Our tendency is to assume that God will use the other guy. Or we just wait for Sister So-and-So to give her regular "Thus saith the Lord" without surrendering ourselves personally to the will and work of the Spirit. We justify turning aside the Spirit's appeal by reminding Him of our inadequacies, inexperience, or lack of qualifications (as if He didn't already know them!). In other instances, we shut our spirit down to the possibility of being used by the Holy Spirit in a supernatural gift. It isn't that we are disobedient, but we are quick to let God know that He had better not ask to use us in a vocal gift. "Don't ask, God, and then I won't have to say no."

But anyone who has ever assumed such a spiritual posture understands how uncomfortable and dissatisfying it is. Our lack of willingness begins to reveal other core issues that need to be dealt with. As a result, our fruitfulness begins to wane. Prayer becomes less intense and productive. Spiritual sensitivities are blunted. Passion ebbs. Enthusiasm diminishes. Service is reduced to mere duty.

How much better it is to say, "Yes, Lord, use me. Yes, Lord, if it is what You desire, let vocal gifts pour through my life." Surrender to His will and enjoy His peace. Whether He chooses to use you in the vocal gifts or not is up to Him. But you are willing.

Yes, Lord, use me.

The positive byproduct is that when He does speak through you, your own life is enriched in Him. Believe that God can use *you* to be the means of encouraging and strengthening the body of Christ.

5

To Speak or Not to Speak

When to Give a Vocal Gift

After answering the question of who should give a supernatural vocal gift in a public service, another question rises. When should a vocal gift be given? What is the Spirit's timing for delivering His message? Is any time a good time as long as the vocal gift is from the Spirit? Am I quenching the Spirit if I "hold" a vocal gift until a particular point in the service?

I was nearing the conclusion of my Sunday morning message, when George (not his real name) leaped to his feet and began to speak in tongues. I knew George well; he was one of our "old-timers" and faithfully attended the church. His motivation was good, and his desire to be used by the Spirit was generally healthy. But he knew better than to interrupt the pastor's message because I had taught him not to do that. Nevertheless here he was, bursting in at an inopportune moment. The congregation was aware of how badly timed the vocal gift was, and you could sense their consternation at what was taking place. But they were also waiting to see what I would do.

Having only seconds to make a decision, I sensed the Holy Spirit giving me direction. So when George finished speaking in tongues, I said, "Let's all hold steady and let the pastor finish his message." You could have heard a pin drop. Speaking in tongues publicly without an interpretation is very much like an unfinished symphony. It leaves you waiting for closure. Tongues and interpretation of tongues operate together; you dare not have one without the other. Yet in this case, I seemed to be asking that tongues not be interpreted.

I tried to pick up the train of thought in my sermon, but I had lost it and so had the people. My mind and the collective thoughts of the congregation were on the interruption. They weren't listening to me any more, but rather were thinking about what had just happened. Quickly, I brought my message to a conclusion, and then began praying.

As I finished my prayer, I felt prompted to say, "If this vocal gift is from the Lord, let's have the interpretation." Immediately, someone gave a strong word that confirmed the message that had been preached. Brother George had indeed given a valid vocal gift of tongues, as was evidenced by the interpretation, but it had simply been given at the wrong time. How much better it would have been to let the preaching of the Word come to its natural conclusion, and then to have given the gift of tongues followed by the interpretation. A clear flow of the Spirit would have been evident to all, and the vocal gifts would have had far greater impact.

Many Spirit-inspired vocal gifts lose their authority because they are poorly timed. The power of their message is dulled because they are given at a point in the service that greatly reduces their effectiveness. Are they inspired of the Spirit—a true word from the Lord for His people? Probably, but because of bad timing they elicit no positive response.

Commonsense Principles

Brother George's story points out that the question of *when* to use a vocal gift can sometimes be answered by knowing *when not* to use one. A supernatural vocal gift should never interrupt Holy Spirit-inspired preaching. It must be acknowledged that some preaching is not always inspiring nor delivered with the Spirit's anointing. But true Pentecostal preaching is modeled after Peter's preaching in the Book of Acts: "Peter, filled with the Holy Spirit, said . . ." (Acts 4:8). A unique filling of the Spirit (we would call it the anointing) enabled Peter to speak with an authority not his own. Would the Spirit then interrupt such preaching with another message? Obviously not. A message in tongues with interpretation or prophecy are supplements to the Word, not substitutes for it. The Scriptures are infallible, but supernatural vocal gifts are not. If we have a choice between which message we should hear, we must always choose the Holy Scriptures. But we are not forced to make that choice. Proper timing of vocal gifts allow for the priority of the preached Word and the strengthening and confirming words of the Spirit.

The same timing issue will keep us from interrupting the reading of God's Word. One of Paul's encouragements to the young pastor, Timothy, was to devote himself to the public reading of Scripture (1 Timothy 4:13). When Jesus preached in His hometown of Nazareth, He began by reading publicly from Isaiah's scroll (Luke 4:16–20). Scripture reading is a common practice in Pentecostal churches because of our commitment to the centrality of the Word. We believe that the Scriptures are inspired by the Holy Spirit, God-breathed, imbued with the divine wind (2 Timothy 3:16; 2 Peter 1:21). So the Spirit will not prompt a vocal gift that would interrupt the powerful Word He has inspired. As we commonly say, the Holy Spirit will not interrupt himself. If the Spirit begins to stir the heart toward giving a supernatural vocal gift, a proper response to that stirring is to wait for an appropriate moment after the reading of the Word to release the gift.

The Holy Spirit will not interrupt himself.

Not interrupting the Word with a vocal gift is a principle not explicitly stated in Scripture. Rather it is a commonsense conclusion that flows from our high value of the Word and its preaching. However, 1 Corinthians 14 does give three clear directives regarding when and when not to use a vocal gift.

Directives from 1 Corinthians 14

First, do not speak in tongues publicly if no interpreter is present at the meeting. "If there is no interpreter, the speaker should keep quiet in the church and speak to himself and God" (1 Corinthians 14:28). This directive underscores Paul's fundamental rule that if vocal gifts are going to edify they must be understandable. His central theme is that prophecy is preferred over uninterpreted tongues because the latter are not understandable to the hearers. Because they are unintelligible, they cannot edify, thus defeating their core purpose. So if a tongues speaker does not know if anyone present is used of God in giving interpretations, he or she should keep silent.

However, Paul offered an alternative to silence. He said, "For this reason"—to build up the church—"anyone who speaks in a tongue should pray that he may interpret what he says" (verse 13). The implication is that God will answer that prayer; the interpretation will be provided by the Spirit and delivered by the tongues speaker with the desired result of the edifying of the body of Christ. But if the person speaking in tongues is unwilling to receive and give the interpretation, and also has no knowledge whether an interpreter is present in the service, then silence is the best course.

A wonderful lady in one of our pastorates was sometimes used of the Spirit to publicly speak in tongues. I say *sometimes* because Sister Alice's (not her real name) tongues were interpreted sometimes, but other times were not. This caused considerable awkwardness and confusion among the people. When I talked with her about it and encouraged her to ask God to give her the interpretation, she said, "Oh, I always pray for the interpretation, but the Lord never gives it to me." I tried to explain that the Scripture would not encourage prayer for the interpretation if God himself were not prepared to answer that prayer. God would subvert His own purposes if He prompted us to pray for an interpretation that He had no intention of giving us. He would not deny us that which He has declared would edify the church. Sister Alice seemed to understand that point, and while I don't recall that she ever gave an interpretation, she was much more sensitive to the need for it.

Paul's second directive regarding when and when not to use a vocal gift restricts the number of tongues and interpretations in a service. "If anyone speaks in a tongue, two—or at the most three—should speak, one at a time, and someone must interpret" (verse 27). The apostle's concern was that tongues, especially without interpretation, were becoming dominant in the church at Corinth. His limitations on the number of vocal gifts of tongues were for the sake of balance. He reminded the Corinthians, "When you come together, everyone has a hymn, or a word of instruction, a revelation, a tongue or an interpretation" (verse 26). In other words, many worship elements, not just tongues and interpretation alone, come together to provide for "the strengthening of the church" (verse 26).

> Needed balance often comes through delineation of boundaries.

Needed balance often comes through delineation of boundaries. Parents provide their children with boundaries, not to be restrictive or to keep their children from enjoying life, but to direct them toward paths that will be full and embracing. Even so, tongues and their interpretation are marvelous tools of blessing, but the Scripture puts boundaries on their use to urge us into other spiritual expressions. Singing, exhortation, praise, preaching, and many other means of worship can provide strength and hope in Christ. We welcome not only the vocal gifts, but other channels of God's grace. Interpreted tongues are just one instrument that adds beauty to the symphony of worship.

Traditionally, Pentecostals have accepted that Paul also limited the number of prophecies in a service. "Two or three prophets should speak, and the others should weigh carefully what is said" (verse 29). Gordon Fee has suggested that since Paul stated in verse 24, "If all prophesy . . ." (KJV, emphasis added), and later added, "You can all prophesy in turn" (verse 31), he was not limiting the number of prophecies in a service. Rather, Paul was saying when two or three prophets have spoken, that is the time to weigh carefully what they have said. [1] Regardless of the view you take, in the context Paul still argued for balance, which if put into practice would disallow the dominance of any one gift, including prophecy.

> *The Spirit does not 'possess' or 'overpower' the speaker.*

The third directive is actually a matter of Christian courtesy in keeping with the principle of order, and could be paraphrased, "Don't all speak at once." Paul said that tongues and interpretation should be given "one at a time" (verse 27). Concerning prophecy he stated, "You can all prophecy in turn" (verse 31). Deference and order are the key elements here.

In this connection Paul wrote, "And if a revelation comes to someone who is sitting down, the first speaker [the person prophesying] should stop" (verse 30). No one person is to control or dominate the service by not allowing others to participate. It is hard for us to imagine that two people might be prophesying simultaneously, but that seems to be what Paul is addressing here. He gives no explanation as to how the first speaker knows that someone else has something to say. Yet no prophecy should be of such length that those who may have a further word do not have opportunity to give it. God desires to use many of His people to bring encouragement to the church.

I have been in worship services when two people began to give an interpretation or a prophecy at exactly the same time. Their first words began simultaneously. Immediately, one would defer to the other. It could be that the same interpretation or prophecy had come to each of them at the same time, but it is more likely that they were separate and different words for the Body that needed to come in turn.

Ecstasy or Control

In all of these directives, Paul assumed that the believer has the capacity to control himself and his speech. If that were not true, the above three directives could not be followed. If personal control is not possible, how could one be silent if no interpreter is present, or speak one at a time, or stop speaking when a revelation comes to someone else?

This control is in contrast to the idea that "the Spirit takes over" and consequently the individual must surrender personal control to the Spirit's power. A spiritual vocal gift is thus equated with an ecstasy that includes giving away control of oneself to the Spirit. I have heard people say, "I just couldn't help myself. I was under the compulsion of the Spirit. I had to speak out when I did. It wasn't my choice." But according to the apostle Paul, that is untrue. "Whatever else, Christian inspiration, including both tongues and prophecy, is not 'out of control.' The Spirit does not 'possess' or 'overpower' the speaker; He is subject to the prophet or tongues-speaker, in the sense that what the Spirit has to say will be said in an orderly and intelligible way. It is indeed the Spirit who speaks, but He speaks through the controlled instrumentality of the believer's own mind and tongue."[2]

It will not be uncommon for a word from God to be received in our spirit during the course of a service to be delivered at some appropriate point later in the service. This does not go against the general Pauline principle of spontaneity of the gifts in public worship. Rather, it aligns itself with Paul's teaching on control and order.

To be under the Spirit's control does not imply that we become out of control. "The spirits of prophets are subject to the control of prophets" (verse 32). Without such control the biblical principle of order (verses 33,40) would be violated.

Understanding for Unbelievers

One of the key questions facing pastors and their congregations is whether or not vocal gifts, especially tongues and interpretation, should be given when unbelievers are present in a church service. In a seeker sensitive church culture, should these gifts be used in more appropriate settings where unchurched people are not present? Since vocal gifts seem to be among the most abused gifts, would it not be better to refrain from their use so that the outsider will not be driven away? Can we avoid causing the unbeliever to think that we are out of our minds? (verse 23). Most importantly, what does the biblical text suggest to help us on this point?

First Corinthians 14 suggests several relevant answers:

1. Tongues without interpretation is a dilemma to both the believer and unbeliever. No one knows what is being said, and consequently the purpose for the vocal gift—edification—is not fulfilled. This goes back to the fundamental and obvious principle that the vocal gifts must be understood to be meaningful. The unchurched person visiting the service may not need edification in the same way a Christian does, but the reality and validity of the gift can be more readily known when what has been said is intelligible.

2. Tongues without interpretation is a negative sign to unbelievers (verse 22). Spirit-filled people nearly always equate "signs" as positive, and in most cases they are. But it seems that in this reference the sign is negative. And it should be emphasized that tongues is not the issue, but rather tongues without an interpretation.

In verse 21, Paul quotes Isaiah 28:11,12, " 'Through men of strange tongues and through the lips of foreigners I will speak to this people, but even then they will not listen to me,' says the

Lord." God sent a foreign army against Israel, a vast horde of warriors who did not speak the native tongue. These people speaking in strange tongues were a sign to Israel of God's impending judgment. Even if they couldn't understand the language, Israel should have gotten the message that judgment was coming. However, they did not understand either the tongue of the foreigners nor the message they brought.

In the same way, an unbeliever may hear tongues spoken in a worship service, but he will not get the "message" unless there is an interpretation. Thus the tongues is a negative sign to the unbeliever, so much so that he will conclude that "you are out of your mind" (verse 23). Israel did not understand God's message because of the hardness of their hearts. The unbeliever does not understand because the message is unintelligible.

3. When everyone speaks in tongues without interpretation, the same conclusion is drawn, "Will they not say that ye are mad?" (verse 23, KJV). Paul described the setting, "So if the whole church comes together and everyone speaks in tongues, and some who do not understand or some unbelievers come in, will they not say that you are out of your mind?" (verse 23). Paul's use of the term "everyone" conjures up images of chaotic tongues speaking without order or control. And those images may not be far from what was occurring in the Corinthian church, hence Paul's words of correction and guidance, not only for the benefit of the church, but also for the benefit of the outsider. Uncontrolled tongues speaking, with or without interpretation, is not the norm for a Spirit-filled church.

4. Tongues with interpretation enables the unbeliever to understand what the Spirit is saying to the congregation. Not allowing tongues and interpretation when visitors are present violates Paul's encouragement, "Do not forbid speaking in tongues" (verse 39). Those who disallow the use of these vocal gifts often cite the need for prophecy since "he who prophesies is greater than the one who

speaks in tongues" (verse 5). However, that misquotes the verse which continues, "unless he interprets, so that the church may be edified." So prophecy is not greater if an interpretation accompanies tongues.

5. However, prophecy is always preferred over tongues without interpretation, because it is understandable and it builds up. "But in the church I would rather speak five intelligible words to instruct others than ten thousand words in a tongue" (verse 19). When one reads the entirety of 1 Corinthians 14, the conclusion is inevitable that

> *Prophecy can provide a clear and certain word from the Lord.*

Paul leaned very much toward the priority of prophecy. He encouraged tongues with interpretation, but prohibited tongues without interpretation. Prophecy can provide a clear and certain word from the Lord.

An Analogy of Waves

A Pentecostal worship service is not unlike the waves of the sea. Small and large waves come at varying intervals. The tide rises and falls. While there is no perfect analogy for Pentecostal worship, these natural phenomena help us understand the waves of the Spirit. Waves of praise in song can crescendo, then fall and ebb. Prayer can begin another wave of blessing as the spiritual tide comes in. The preaching of the Word is like a wave that begins far from shore but gradually grows until it comes to fullness.

The time to give a supernatural vocal gift is not when a wave is at its peak. For instance, united, corporate verbal praise can crescendo to a peak. That is not when a vocal gift should be given, because it will break into what God is already doing. People will stop verbalizing praise to listen to the vocal gift. Wait until the praise subsides, the wave crashes, and a pause comes in the service. *That* is the time to give a vocal gift, because when the Spirit authors it, the exercise of the vocal gift will create another wave of glory and blessing. Many times I have been in services where there have been multiple vocal gifts interspersed with singing, corporate praise, exhortation, testimony, and each one was like another wave washing over the congregation in refreshing, cleansing power.

The person leading the service plays an essential role in encouraging a pause between waves. Pentecostals are often uncomfortable with any hesitations in the service. Before a wave has fully subsided, we are singing another chorus, giving an exhortation, or moving on to another part of the service. We do not allow for moments when vocal gifts from the Spirit can be given without seeming interruption. If we want the vocal gifts to be active and alive in our services, we must sometimes wait for them. This allows opportunity for those whom God uses to respond to the urgings of the Spirit at the appropriate moment.

In churches where the leadership screens vocal gifts prior to their being given, the timing of the vocal gift is left, not to the person using the gift, but to the one leading the service. Not only can that leader provide an appropriate moment for the vocal gift to be given,

The person leading the service plays an essential role.

but the leader can prepare the people for it through a brief word of introduction and instruction.

I was visiting a church in the Midwest, and was greatly blessed by the heartfelt worship and the expository message. When the pastor had finished preaching, he made an altar appeal, and a large number of people responded. We continued to sing worshipfully, and the pastor asked again for an altar response, and another wave of people came to pray. After another worshipful pause, the benediction was given, but as soon as the final "Amen" was said, a vocal gift of tongues came forth and a powerful interpretation followed.

From our limited perspective, we could have thought that God had finished His work because the benediction had been given. But as He often does, the Holy Spirit surprised us by pressing past human boundaries to finish His work. The pastor cooperated with the Spirit by handling the unusual situation with spiritual sensitivity. He said something to the effect that, "It is obvious that we thought the service was over, but the Holy Spirit still has more that He wants to do today. We want Him to complete His work, and the interpretation demands a response from us." He proceeded to give a third appeal to come and seek God at the altars and many more responded. Such was the flow of the Spirit that no one spoke out of turn, no correction was needed, and each part of the service contributed strength and blessing. Jesus was exalted, and the church was built up. What was clearly supernatural had become the expected and welcomed norm for God's people.

If the Lord has a word to speak through you, always be obedient, but also be sensitive as to when to speak. When delivered at the right moment, the vocal gift will accomplish its desired end— the building up of Christ's Church.

Endnotes

[1] Gordon Fee, *The New International Commentary on the New Testament: The First Epistle to the Corinthians.* (Grand Rapids: Eerdmans, 1987), 693–696.

[2] Fee, 692.

6

Can You Hear Me Now?

How a Vocal Gift Should Be Given

I was attending an old-fashioned summer camp meeting when a man about two rows behind me began to prophesy. Such vocal gifts were a normal part of the camp services, but the manner in which the vocal gift started was definitely unusual. The brother began his "message" with a mighty "AHA!" bellowed at the top of his lungs. I just about jumped out of my skin, and everyone else within ten rows was equally startled. The rest of the prophecy was then given in a more customary fashion though still at the highest possible decibel level. The only thing I remember about the vocal gift now is "Aha!" The content of that prophecy had little or no impact because of the manner in which it was given.

How should a vocal gift be given? Is it necessary to use King James English? Will people be able to hear? Should interpretations and prophecies always be prefaced with, "Thus saith the Lord"? Grammatically, should the first person or the third person be used? What about the tone of voice? Is the force of the message somehow lost if a microphone is used? Does the Bible give us any guidance on these questions?

The Scripture does not directly address all these issues. Some points are implied by the biblical text, but in most cases experience and wisdom need to be applied. The fact that the Bible is mostly silent may indicate that the *how* of giving vocal gifts is not at the highest level of importance. Certainly, it is not as critical as the *what* of the message. And yet, anything that detracts the hearer from listening, not only with the ears, but with the heart should be eliminated if possible.

Normal Voice

The "Aha" brother did not understand that a message given in a normal tone of voice could be as effective as one delivered at ear-shattering levels. In fact, it would have been more effective because people would have concentrated on the words instead of the sound.

The volume level of vocal gifts was not an issue in the house churches in Corinth. They never faced the challenge of large sanctuaries and even larger auditoriums. For them very little volume was needed to give vocal gifts. However, in today's larger settings it is important to raise one's voice sufficiently so that people can hear. Some church fellowships will place microphones strategically throughout large auditoriums for people to use. Others will wait for the leader to give them the release to speak, often from the platform, using amplification. Then the vocal gifts can be given in a normal, conversational manner and tone.

I have attended Charismatic conferences in large arenas where many thousands of people were in attendance. A vocal gift has been given from the second or third balcony, but those on the other side of the arena were not able to hear. So instead of the vocal gift being a powerful encouragement to the people, it actually put a damper on the spirit of the service. People wanted to respond to what was said, but could not because they were not able to hear. Previously, we discussed the Pauline principle of intelligibility, and unless people can hear, they will not be able to understand.

Normal Language

In years past, it was customary to hear interpretations and prophecies given in what we call King James English. In other words, the same language used in the King James Version of the Bible was used to deliver vocal gifts. *Thee* and *thou* were frequent. Most verbs ended in *th*, as in "Thus saith the Lord." Some have been intimidated by the King James factor and have been hesitant to speak because they could not conform to this manner of speaking.

The good news is that God can deliver His message through normal language. Our customary vernacular does not have to change. God uses us as we are, and we do not have to become a different person, albeit Spirit-empowered, to be used by Him. Besides, other people can understand it better when we speak in everyday language.

Emotional Control

While using a vocal gift, some on occasion will be overcome with emotion, usually in the form of weeping. Their words are punctuated by deep sobs, perhaps prompted by deep compassion or godly sorrow. Their brokenness says much about the heart of the person and their sensitivity to the Spirit. They are delivering God's message with tenderness of spirit.

However, when the person becomes so overcome by weeping that he or she has difficulty enunciating the words prompted by the Spirit, then those listening cannot adequately receive the word from the Lord. I have heard valid uses of the vocal gifts, but the people were so emotional that I could understand only a part of what they were saying.

We certainly do not encourage cold, emotionless vocal gifts. Emotions, whether sorrow or joy, can add impact and power to the message. Nevertheless, the speaker must control his emotions sufficiently so that he can speak in a clear and understandable manner.

To God or the Church?

This question deals only with a vocal gift of tongues and its interpretation. Prophecy is not in view, except as it may provide contrast.

Some feel quite strongly that an interpretation should be spoken in the form of prayer, addressed directly to God and not to the congregation. They buttress their position with these key verses from 1 Corinthians 14:

- "For anyone who speaks in a tongue does not speak to men but to God" (verse 2).
- "If I pray in a tongue, my spirit prays" (verse 14).
- "If you are praising God with your spirit" (verse 16).
- "You may be giving thanks well enough" (verse 17).

Consequently, the argument is made that if the essence of the tongues gift is prayer, praise, and thanksgiving, then the interpretation that gives the meaning of the tongue will also be in the form of prayer. Therefore, the interpretation will not be addressed to the

The interpretation is not a translation of the tongue, but a giving of the sense or meaning of the tongue.

congregation as a message or word to them from the Lord.

This is not the generally accepted understanding of the gift of interpretation. Usually, we look for it to contain a message from the Lord for His people or for unbelievers. So how do we respond to this perception of the Scripture?

First, it is possible to miss the distinction Paul makes between the private use of tongues in prayer, i.e., our prayer language which requires no interpretation, and the public use of the gift of tongues that mandates an interpretation. It seems to me that the verses cited above, and the arguments that come from them, mix the two applications of tongues.

Second, the interpretation is not a translation of the tongues, but a giving of the sense or meaning of the tongues. So even if a prayer is offered to God in tongues, the meaning and significance of that to the hearers may not be in the form of prayer. For instance, the prayer in tongues may extol God's faithfulness: "God, you are faithful." But the interpreter in giving the meaning of that prayer may put it in a declarative form: "God is faithful." The tongues speaker is certainly correct in praising God for His faithfulness. But the interpreter is also correct in affirming to the church that God is faithful. And the church is strengthened and edified by the tongues and interpretation.

So in my opinion, the interpreter should not be bound to expressing the interpretation in the form of prayer, but may address it as a message that the Lord wants the congregation to hear.

The Third Person

Confusion and misunderstanding can be avoided when one speaks using the third person rather than the first. By the third person we mean using *He*, in contrast to using the first person *I*. Examples of giving an interpretation or a prophecy in the first person would be:

- Thus saith the Lord, I love you with an everlasting love.
- I, the Lord your God, say to you that I am in your midst today.

Giving a vocal gift in the third person, one might say:

- The Lord would say that He loves you with an everlasting love.
- Hear the word of the Lord: He is saying that He is in your midst today.

Does it make any difference whether you use the first or third person? I believe it does for two primary reasons:

First, speaking in the first person implies infallibility. Whenever "Thus saith the Lord" is used, the speaker is purporting to say exactly what God would say if He were present and speaking. God never misspeaks. Everything He says is true. However, the potential for prophecies to be fallible is implied when Paul says, "Two or three prophets should speak, and the others should weigh carefully what is said" (1 Corinthians 14:29). No such admonition would be given if error were not possible. Those of us who have been around Pentecostal and Charismatic circles for a while can attest that some vocal gifts not only contain error, but are completely invalid.

Only the Scripture is infallible and inerrant. Vocal gifts were never intended to be raised to the authority level of the Bible. Scripture is the first and last standard by which the very best of vocal gifts are to be judged.

A variation from the third to the first person might be necessary if a prophecy is predictive. Since predictive prophecy is judged by whether the prophecy comes to pass, it must always be infallible. Therefore, it is of little consequence whether the first or third person is used. Agabus's prophecy concerning Paul's future was prefaced by, "The Holy Spirit says" (Acts 21:11). That he was a true prophet was attested by the fact that the prophecy concerning Paul came to pass.

Second, speaking in the first person can confuse unbelievers. I had never considered this until an incident took place during my college years that gave me a broader perspective. The Bible college students had a favorite hamburger restaurant they often frequented after church services. They had targeted one of the waiters for special "witnessing" attention. One evening, I heard him talking to one of his fellow workers, and realized from the conversation that he had finally attended a service with one of the students. I was delighted, until I heard what he related that had occurred during the service.

He said to his friend, "You will never guess what happened tonight. It was unbelievable! A man got up in the middle of the service, and actually said he was God." I immediately knew what had happened. Someone had given an interpretation or prophecy using first person terminology, "I am the Lord thy God, and I say to thee. . . ." To a lifelong Pentecostal like me, that would be pretty normal terminology, but to the unbelieving waiter, it was shocking enough that to my knowledge he never went back to church again. That is not the outcome we are looking for. We do not want the method of giving a vocal gift to obscure the message, and confuse the unbeliever.

A vocal gift and its delivery could be compared to a jewel and its setting. The setting exists only to enhance the beauty of the jewel. If attention is drawn to the setting rather than the jewel, then the focus is wrong and the magnificence of the jewel is overshadowed. In the same way, a vocal gift must be delivered in a manner that serves only to focus people's attention on the message. The method of delivery should not distract from that which the Spirit desires to communicate.

7

Testing, Discerning, and Spiritual Perception

How to Judge a Vocal Gift

It seems surprising that gifts originating with the Holy Spirit and supernaturally bestowed on the believer should need to be assessed and evaluated, but they do. By carefully listening to each vocal gift, we can determine if affirmation or correction is needed. This is not done arbitrarily, but follows the guidance of Scripture: "Two or three prophets should speak, and the others should weigh carefully what is said" (1 Corinthians 14:29). This has primary application to a prophetic word, but the same careful assessments should be made of interpretations of tongues. The King James Version uses the terminology of judging what is said, but not in the sense of being critical or condemning. Rather, it is listening and evaluating the content of the message.

Who are the "others" who are to do the judging? We are not told specifically, and some would assign this to other prophets. But in context, it would seem to be the hearers. All Spirit-filled believers are given capacities of judgment if they will use and refine them. However, a special burden for weighing the validity of a vocal gift rests on the leader/pastor. Even if the pastor is not on the platform when a vocal gift occurs, he or she carries primary responsibility for the ministry of correction. The pastor may trust the leader of the service to weigh what is said and make appropriate comments or corrections, but he is still responsible for them. Even if the whole congregation judges the vocal gift to be wrong, they are not in a position to provide correction, especially public correction. The pastor fills that role.

We are always conscious of the biblical warning, "Do not put out the Spirit's fire; do not treat prophecies with contempt" (1 Thessalonians 5:19,20). Or as the King James Version puts it, "Quench not the Spirit. Despise not prophesyings." Our judgment of vocal gifts is not for the purpose of quenching what the Spirit is doing, but to encourage His mighty works. It is worth noting that after this warning we are told, "Test everything. Hold on to the good. Avoid every kind of evil" (verses 21,22). While it is possible to be so judgmental in a negative sense that we stifle the Spirit's work, it is also possible to put out His fire by failing to test everything.

Objective truth should be utilized to make assessments.

It is interesting that the phrase in 1 Corinthians 14:29, "weigh carefully what is said," uses the same verb found in the expression "discerning of spirits" (1 Corinthians 12:10, KJV) or "distinguishing between spirits" (NIV), which is one of the nine supernatural gifts. The same discerning ability used to know whether certain spirits are of God or not also helps us determine the validity of a vocal gift.[1] We should not conclude from this that judging a prophetic word always involves distinguishing between demonic spirits and the Holy Spirit, but the same ability given by the Spirit is at work. While aspects of judgment are subjective, wherever possible, objective truth should also be utilized to make assessments.

And yet we must acknowledge that the Scripture itself does not establish clear criteria for judging vocal gifts. We often wish that it did. So the following is presented as the product of practical experience and the study of biblical principles. And we should note again that the biblical encouragement to "weigh carefully what is said" is applicable only to prophecy. However, since tongues and interpretation, like prophecy, are to build up the church, it may be assumed that they too should be weighed using a similar standard.

The Word of God

The first objective criterion for judging an interpretation or prophecy is, Does the content of the message align itself with the Word of God? If it does not, we immediately discount it as a valid Spirit-inspired vocal gift. It may not be from the devil, but is more likely to have come from the mind of the speaker. We can be thankful that vocal gifts contradicting the Word are rare. Nevertheless the infallible Scripture is our standard of truth. "A modern prophetic vocal gift can legitimately neither contradict nor add to the Word." [2]

A pastor friend of mine told me about a lady who had recently given a prophecy in his church which began, "As Cat in the Hat would say." And then she proceeded to give the vocal gift in rhyme. After that auspicious beginning, it really didn't matter much what the content of the message was. It was invalid, because Dr. Seuss is not the source of supernatural vocal gifts. The whole thing was so obviously absurd, even humorous, that the pastor didn't feel like he needed to say anything publicly to correct it. Cat in the Hat does not line up well with the Word!

The Fruit Produced by Vocal Gifts

While the general principles of the Word give us guidance, it also makes clear that good fruit will be produced in the church by tongues, interpretation, and prophecy. Their effect on the people should be to strengthen, encourage, comfort, and edify them (1 Corinthians 14:3,4). If they tend to beat down, castigate, and upbraid God's people, they are not inspired of the Spirit. They may include correction, because that can strengthen the body of Christ. Even a note of impending judgment may edge in, but it must not be given with a harshness that implies the speaker is happy about coming doom, or thinks his hearers deserve it. The overall impact of these gifts must always be to build up and strengthen.

Peter set forth another standard for prophecy. "And we have the word of the prophets made more certain, and you will do well to pay attention to it, as to a light shining in a dark place, until the day dawns and the morning star rises in your hearts" (2 Peter 1:19). What a beautiful description of the prophetic word—a

Prophecy has Jesus at its heart and center.

light shining in a dark place. So we can expect prophecy to illuminate, provide insight, and enlighten. By contrast if it is not a true word from the Lord, it may bring darkness and despondency to the spirit, or at the least fail to lift the darkness.

Then John the Revelator gave us this standard that defines the essence of prophecy. "For the testimony of Jesus is the spirit of prophecy" (Revelation 19:10). Prophecy has Jesus at its heart and center.

A Christian acquaintance of mine felt that he and his wife had received some prophetic insights regarding a particular church. They had delivered these prophecies in various church services, and had also written them down.[3] Since I had a relationship with that congregation, he felt it would be helpful for me to have copies to read. I believe he was sincere in his desire to help the church. But when I read through the prophecies, my immediate conclusion was, "There's no 'Jesus' in them." They were mostly blood, thunder, and dire warnings, but offered little hope. These purported prophecies were full of darkness, but never turned on the light. They never pointed the church to the answer to its dilemma—Jesus. I concluded that as sincere as these friends were, their vocal gifts were not from the Lord.

The Ring of Authority

Is the vocal gift given with an authority that can only come from the Holy Spirit? This, of course, is a very subjective judgment. So another way of putting it might be, Does it witness with our spirit? Like two sides of a coin, the speaker must deliver the vocal gift in the authority of the Spirit, and when that happens, my spirit is quick to say, "Amen." The hearer cannot create the authority, but can only attest to it.

Some vocal gifts certainly do not contradict the Word, nor do they drag us into darkness. But neither do they lift our hearts toward God. They may be a hodgepodge of religious phrases thrown together or a tiresome litany of repetitive exhortations. They weary the hearers, who can hardly wait until the whole unseemly "word" is over. No fresh insight. No illuminating encouragement. No ring of authority. It does not meet the standard.

The Flow of the Service

Is the vocal gift in keeping with the general tenor of the service? For instance, if an evident spirit of joy is in the worship, and the Spirit is leading God's people to rejoice, a vocal gift on the responsibility to reach the lost would seem out of place. Or if the service is given over to a missions theme and emphasizing the church's responsibility to reach lost people, a word on rejoicing would be inconsistent with the flow. That doesn't mean these vocal gifts would not have a valid point, and perhaps later in the service the emphasis might change and then that word could more appropriately be given. This is usually an issue of timing more than anything else.

Occasionally while in my private devotions, I have had the Lord drop a prophetic word in my heart that I realized was not only for me, but for the church. All I had to do was wait, and an appropriate moment in a future service would come for me to give that word. I have never sensed, "This word is for next Sunday morning." I have only been aware that when the time was right, the Spirit would prompt me to deliver it, and He has been faithful to do so. The right moment is when the flow of the service and the prophetic word are consistent.

These on-the-spot assessments of the speaking gifts are challenging. Yet, they provide opportunities. On the one hand, we can affirm what is said and encourage a response. On the other hand, we can offer kind correction that will strengthen both the speaker and the congregation.

Endnotes

[1] Fee, 596,597.

[2] L. Thomas Holdcroft, *The Holy Spirit: A Pentecostal Interpretation.* (Springfield, MO: Gospel Publishing House, 1979), 173.

[3] The Bible does not prohibit writing vocal gifts down. However, the danger in doing so is that some may attempt to elevate them to the level of Scripture.

8

Keeping the River
in Its Banks

When Correction Is Needed

Wouldn't it be wonderful if all tongues, interpretations, and prophecies were right on, and were given at the perfect moment in all our services by saints who were not only articulate, but godly as well? That is a pastor's dream. But alas, it is just a dream. The reality is that God uses people who have flaws and imperfections, which means that their ministries, supernatural or not, will also be flawed. On occasion, they may need correction through the Spirit and the Word, but God may also use their pastor for that same purpose.

That was the case when an elderly minister named Leonard (not his real name) began attending our church. Occasionally, he would give a message in tongues and then without taking a breath, launch into the interpretation. At first, these vocal gifts seemed to be fairly normal, but over time their sameness became evident. It wasn't that the interpretations were doctrinally off, but neither did they contain a substantive message for the people. They lacked the Spirit's authority and anointing. The repetitiveness of the words eventually dulled the ears and hearts of the congregation, so they stopped listening. I knew something had to be done.

As the pastor, my challenge was to know how to correct the situation. I wanted to exhibit the spirit Paul talked about when he said, "Do not rebuke an older man harshly, but exhort him as if he were your father" (1 Timothy 5:1). After all, this good brother had been in the ministry more years than I had been alive!

I decided to visit him at his home, endeavoring to deal privately with the issue, and thus not embarrass him publicly. I gently said to him, "Leonard, I had some real questions about the vocal gift you gave this past Sunday." To my surprise he said, "You know, so did I." That opened up a long dialogue in which I encouraged him to give others an opportunity to be used. By not pausing between the tongues and the interpretation, he was not giving even the Lord an option as to whom He would use. In addition, we discussed the purpose and value of the vocal gifts, and the need for them to edify and build up.

For several weeks, he did not give a vocal gift. I was relieved and felt that we had solved a problem in a way that continued to honor Leonard as an elder in the faith. However, one Sunday morning he came into the service very late, while I was giving the altar appeal. I later learned he had been part of our prayer team that met to pray for the service. He had no idea what was happening in the service, but proceeded to give his usual message in tongues followed immediately by the interpretation. When he finished, I said to the congregation, "That had nothing to do with what God is doing in the service this morning. Let's continue to follow His leadership." And I continued with the altar call. Our people were so attuned to what the Spirit was doing that my comments dismissing his vocal gift were accepted without hesitation. Later, I went to Leonard and let him know why I said what I did. As one might expect from this stalwart saint, he accepted my correction with grace. This was a case where private correction worked for a time, but public correction was required in order to maintain the flow of the Spirit in the worship service.

Preventive Measures

Pastors can save themselves a lot of time and challenge if they will initiate measures that will avoid the necessity of corrective action. Primary among those preventatives is clear biblical teaching. It is far better to teach your people how to use the gifts correctly than to be forced to correct believers for using the gifts wrongly. I have already emphasized the teaching responsibilities of the pastor, and do not want to belabor the point. But I do want to underscore it as a significant factor in averting the need for correction.

Key teaching moments are presented every time a vocal gift is given. When the vocal gift is finished and the response of the congregation has subsided, the pastor can give a brief explanation of what has just taken place. [1] That might include several details, such as:

- Affirming our belief in the supernatural for this and every generation
- Stressing the value and importance of the supernatural gifts for the church today
- Emphasizing the need to hear a fresh word from the Lord in keeping with the Scripture
- Giving a biblical explanation of what type of gift was used, and what its purpose is
- Validating the specific word that was given and its application to the congregation

All of this can be done in a minute or two. It doesn't require a long and drawn-out explanation. But when these capsulated teachings are done consistently over time, they become a strong preventative against misuse of the gifts. (The Appendix includes some examples of what might be said following specific vocal gifts.)

These teaching moments do not take the place of regular and consistent teaching about the vocal gifts. Classes or small groups settings where the teacher and students can engage in dialogue and where questions and answers can be exchanged are invaluable. But the public worship service provides the advantage of addressing the whole church, and not just a smaller group.

Correction or Rebuke

What if a vocal gift is given, and we endeavor to weigh carefully what is said, but it does not seem to measure up. We bring correction then and there, right? To which we answer a clear and decisive, "Maybe." So much depends on what was said, the circumstances of the service, the person giving the vocal gift, and other factors, not the least of which is the Spirit leading us to know how to respond in that moment. No simple *Vocal Gifts Playbook for Dummies* is available to tell us what to do. But we are not alone. We have the Holy Spirit to help us.

We first must accept that part of the pastor's function is to give correction. We know that preaching the Word involves correction, rebuke, and encouragement. While correction of those using the vocal gifts is not a preaching moment, they will still need at various times to be encouraged, rebuked, and corrected. Correction is not as harsh as rebuke. It realigns, puts back on course, reestablishes spiritual focus, and gives direction. Correction has a strong teaching element in that it not only points out what is wrong, but provides instruction on how to do things right. It requires much patience, repetition, and grace.

Public Correction

When the need for correction is obvious, should it be offered in front of the congregation or to the individual in private? It depends on the nature of the offense. With some exceptions, public correction should not be given until efforts at private correction have failed. Nevertheless, the pastor keeps in focus his responsibility for both the speaker and the congregation. Efforts to affirm the person while dealing with the issue are commendable. But the guarding of the congregation is also a high priority, even if it means that the feelings of the speaker may be hurt.

Some of the reasons public correction might be needed are:

- Contradiction of the doctrine, principles, and facts of Scripture. A good example would be a prophecy that predicts when Jesus will return for His Church.
- Misrepresentation of the character of God. For instance, God may be portrayed as harsh, angry, and lacking in compassion without reference to the fact that nothing can separate us from His love.
- Presenting an unbalanced truth. This is similar to the previous point and could be illustrated by a vocal gift that declares the inevitability of future judgment, but fails to balance that message with the present mercies of God. In some cases, this kind of message may have been cut short before the entire word was given. In such cases, I have sometimes said, "I believe God has more to say to us, so let's just wait for Him to speak." Then usually someone else would give the balancing word.
- When vocal gifts exceed in number the biblical maximums. For tongues and interpretations, the maximum is three (1 Corinthians 14:27). For prophecies, it is generally accepted that the maximum is also three (verse 29). When vocal gifts go beyond that, it is wise to stop them as soon as they start.
- When there is no interpretation of tongues. It is always appropriate to wait for the interpretation and not be in a hurry to move on in the service. Where the tongues speaker has been taught to pray for the interpretation, the pastor may simply call on him to do so. Other times, when it becomes obvious that the interpretation is not going to be forthcoming, an appropriate comment needs to be made. It may be in the form of teaching about what should have happened, but didn't.
- When private correction has failed. Most people are willing to receive private correction and amend their vocal gifts

accordingly. But if they persist in giving inept, inadequate, and inappropriate vocal gifts, then public correction is required.

Public correction does not always have to follow immediately after the vocal gift is given. An interval in the service can help the pastor formulate a response. When done later, the correction will seem more generalized and not specifically aimed at the speaker.

Sometimes a pastor cannot wait to intervene until a vocal gift is finished. What is being said, and the spirit in which it is said, is so obviously bad that it must be stopped. Or maybe the timing of the vocal gift interrupts a powerful flow of the Spirit and needs to be curtailed. In these cases, the pastor must take immediate, decisive action, depending wholly on the leadership of the Holy Spirit in what to say and how to say it.

Private Correction

Correction of Christians in private provides the pastor the opportunity not only to provide gentle instruction, but to assess their attitudes and spirits. In particular, the pastor is on the alert for a teachable spirit, the attitude of heart that welcomes correction as a means of growth. Such a person understands the Bible principle: "Whoever heeds correction gains understanding" (Proverbs 15:32). Usually that is what the pastor will find, but not always.

Debbie (not her real name) had been attending our church for a while, and had been used of God in prophecy. Though somewhat strident at times, the vocal gifts for the most part were valid. Then one Sunday morning, she gave a blistering prophecy (I hesitate to call it prophecy) that was clearly aimed at her unsaved husband sitting next to her. Her words were angry, accusing, mean, and hurtful. A guest evangelist was in the pulpit, and he quickly moved on with the service. Looking back now, if I had it to do over, I would have gone to the platform to immediately offer a word of correction.

After prayer, my wife and I went that week to visit Debbie at her home. When I raised the possibility that maybe her prophecies were being clouded by her personal feelings about her husband's unconverted status, she exploded. How could I dare question what God had given her? Why didn't I recognize the gift of God within her? What right did I have to challenge a word from the Lord? Judi and I left with heavy hearts. Debbie never returned to our church.

But what was even sadder was that her husband never came back either. He was not far from the Kingdom. I had developed a good relationship with him, and was sure that in time I would win him to Christ. The lack of a teachable spirit may have kept Debbie from receiving what she wanted most—the salvation of her husband. Had she been open to correction, what a difference it would have made.

The occasions for private correction are so numerous that we cannot possible deal with all of them. Some of the more obvious instances would include the following:

- When things are done out of ignorance. This is a great teaching opportunity. Many well-meaning, rightly motivated people do wrong things. Most of them are not so problematic that they must be dealt with publicly, but certainly we can help such people learn and grow from their mistakes.

  A young lady began handing me written prophecies she felt the Lord had given her. Without any explanation from her, I was left to read them and discover that they were in essence, uttering curses, calling down the fires of judgment on our church, and issuing it dire warnings. To her credit, she came to see me to discover my reaction to them. When told that they may have come from her own spirit and not the Holy Spirit, she was quick to defend herself. She explained that she just wrote down what the Holy Spirit told her, and she was not responsible for what was said. She saw herself as an automaton through which the Spirit poured His words into her pen and onto paper. My response was that the speaker or writer is always responsible for the message he delivers, and that we are not automatons without a will. Her written prophecies as well as her defense of them came from an ignorance of the Spirit's work in relationship to the human will.

- When bad habits have developed. Bad habits in delivering vocal gifts may include repetition of words and phrases, an unnatural tone of voice, invariably speaking at the wrong time, or repeating what was said last time. We can't nitpick at people on some of these points, and the Lord must help us decide if and when to say anything.

- When a person's life is known to be inconsistent with his message. This is not a call to perfection by the speakers. However, if a person is known to be living a sinful lifestyle but is allowed to give vocal gifts, it reflects badly on the pastoral leadership and confuses the congregation. This may indeed be a situation that calls for public correction, and a refusal to allow the person to speak at all in the congregational setting. This is one reason why some local churches do not allow guests to give vocal gifts, but only members.

In cases calling for private correction, I have often asked the Lord to give me a natural opening to talk to the person in question. The best scenario is for them to initiate the conversations. But barring that, no one wants to call someone "on the carpet." Confrontation is not the goal, but correction is. How much better it is when the Spirit creates openings for correction and teaching. But if they do not come as naturally as we would like, we will still need to meet privately with the person to work through the exact issues.

Responding to Correction

So what if you are the one who "messed up" when using a vocal gift? You are sincere in your desire to be used by God, but you have blurted out at inopportune times in a service, or given messages from your own spirit rather than the Holy Spirit. You've been embarrassed and humiliated when the pastor had to publicly correct the vocal gifts you have given. What hope is there for the person whose heart is right, but who still misuses the gifts?

Don't be disheartened! God can still use you. He has not given up on you. However, your need for correction means you still have some maturing to do in relationship to the Spirit's work. Errors in substance and delivery do not disqualify you from future manifestation of the gifts, but you need to grow.

Receive with grace and submission the correction that is offered. Remain under the spiritual authority of your pastor. Maintain a humble and teachable spirit. Acknowledge your blunders and ask God to help you be more sensitive to His voice. Engage in a serious and detailed study of 1 Corinthians 14. Read all you can about the gifts of tongues, interpretation, and prophecy. Seek out those who are effective in these gifts. Ask for their counsel and direction. Stay open to the Holy Spirit.

Many of God's great leaders made mistakes for which they needed correction and discipline, but they were better leaders for it. No one is above correction. We all need it, and when we receive it as from the Lord, we become better Christians, and more effective in gift ministry.

Endnote

[1] See the Appendix for examples of what could be said for specific situations when vocal gifts are used.

Appendix

Examples of What Could Be Said Following Tongues, Interpretation of Tongues, or Prophecy

"Some of our guests today may be unfamiliar with what just happened. The Bible refers to the gifts of different kinds of tongues and the interpretation of those tongues. That's what we have heard today. This is one of the ways God has designed to continue to speak to His church. You can read more about them in 1 Corinthians 12 and 14. This morning, through these gifts we have been encouraged to . . ." (Then give the essence of the interpretation and encourage a response.)

"At XYZ Church we believe in the supernatural. We believe God still uses His people in supernatural ways. That's what He has done this morning. You can read about tongues in the Book of Acts, and about tongues and interpretation in 1 Corinthians. These gifts functioned in the Early Church, and we believe that, just as that generation needed these spoken gifts, our generations needs them today. The exhortation we have heard was to . . ." (Give the essence of the word given and its application.)

"God is a communicating God. He speaks to His people. Sometimes it's in our hearts, through our conscience, through nature, and even through other people. When God breaks through the speech barrier, we need to hear what He has to say. He has spoken today through a clear word of prophecy, which is to strengthen, encourage, and comfort us. We believe His communication today urges us to . . ." (Elaborate on the content.)

"We believe in what the Bible calls the gifts of the Spirit. Some of these work silently and behind the scenes—gifts such as prayer and hospitality—but others are vocal and are to be heard by the whole church. In your Bible, 1 Corinthians 14 in particular, you will discover these vocal gifts and how they are to be used. God has used two of our people today to speak forth in an unknown language and then interpret it for our benefit. The language is supernatural and the interpretation is given without forethought by the speaker. God knew what we needed today and encouraged us with . . ." (Give specifics of the word.)

"How many believe in the supernatural? Oh yes, we believe God still does miracles because Jesus Christ is the same yesterday, today, and forever. The spoken gift of prophecy that we have heard today is supernatural in origin. It is one way God continues to speak to His church. And we need Him to speak. We need to hear what He has to say to us. We are strengthened and encouraged by this word from the Lord, which has urged us to . . ." (State core truth of the vocal gift.)

Examples of What Could Be Said When an Interpretation Did Not Follow Tongues

"We believe in the gifts of the Spirit, and in the gift of tongues which we have heard today. But when a vocal gift of tongues is given, it must always be accompanied by an interpretation. The object of the gifts is to strengthen and build up the body of Christ, but that can't happen when tongues alone are heard, because we don't understand them. They need an interpretation understood by all. That's why the Bible in 1 Corinthians 14 says that the one who speaks in tongues should pray that he or she would receive the interpretation. Let's remember that just because the gifts may be used imperfectly sometimes, it does not mean we should not allow their use at all. Let's continue to grow in our understanding of how to be used of God in the gift ministry."

"We have just heard a vocal gift of tongues. We know from Scripture that tongues without interpretation is not the proper function of that gift. That does not always mean that the tongues were not from the Lord. It may mean the person who was to give the interpretation did not obey. It could mean that the tongues speaker was offering praise to God, but it should not have been given to the whole congregation. It might also mean that the person speaking in tongues should have been quiet, because no interpreter is present. Whatever the case, we have not received the full benefit of this gift, because it was not interpreted so that we could be strengthened in our faith. In spite of our frailties and mistakes, God will be faithful to continue to speak to us."

"In the New Testament book of 1 Corinthians we have guidelines for supernatural vocal gifts. There is one cardinal rule for the gift of tongues that we have heard today and that is, it must be interpreted. That didn't happen so none of us could benefit from what the interpretation would have said to us. If no interpreter is present, then the person should not give the vocal gift of tongues or he or she should be prepared to give the interpretation. So for the benefit of the church, we would ask the person who gave the vocal gift of tongues to now give the interpretation."

"The Bible says that when we speak in tongues, we are really speaking to God. For instance, in our private devotions we might speak in tongues as a regular part of our prayer life, but such tongues are not interpreted. In a public service, when those tongues are for the whole church, then they need to be interpreted. However, sometimes we don't know the difference between the private and public use, and we say publicly what should have been kept private. That's what I believe happened just now. Personal prayer overflowed in the public setting. This vocal gift was not for the church, so shouldn't have been given. Because of that, there was no interpretation."

Examples of What Could Be Said in Public Correction

"We are people of the Word and the Spirit. We greatly value the gifts of the Spirit, but first we bow to the authority of the Scripture. It is our final rule for faith and conduct. And Paul taught us in 1 Corinthians 14 that in our services there should never be more than three tongues and interpretations (or prophecies). We appreciate the motivation of the speaker, but nevertheless we want to follow the guidelines of God's Word."

"We are a Pentecostal church, and we appreciate the gifts of the Spirit and encourage their use. But all supernatural vocal gifts are to be judged by the Word. And one thing that was said about God does not match what the Scriptures say about Him. (Point out the error, and contrast it with Scripture.) We are always in good order to stick to what the Scripture says."

"My brother (or sister), please don't interrupt. This is not the time to give a vocal gift. The Holy Spirit is speaking through His Word. That is what needs to be heard right now. I know you want to help, but let the pastor finish his message." (Keep preaching!)

Bibliography

Basham, Don. *A Handbook on Tongues, Interpretation, and Prophecy.* Monroeville, PA: Whitaker Books, 1971.

Bennett, Dennis and Rita Bennett. *The Holy Spirit and You: A Study Guide to the Spirit-filled Life.* Gainesville, FL: Bridge-Logos, 1971.

Brandt, R. L. *Tongues: The Greatest Gift.* South Plainfield, NJ: Bridge Publishing, 1981.

Fee, Gordon D. *God's Empowering Presence: The Holy Spirit in the Letters of Paul.* Peabody, MA: Hendrickson Publishers, 1994.

_____. *Paul, the Spirit, and the People of God.* Peabody, MA: Hendrickson Publishers, 1996.

_____. *The New International Commentary on the New Testament: The First Epistle to the Corinthians.* Grand Rapids, MI: Eerdmans, 1987.

Gee, Donald. *Concerning Spiritual Gifts.* Springfield, MO: Gospel Publishing House, 1949.

Hayford, Jack. *Living the Spirit Formed Life.* Ventura, CA: Regal Books, 2001.

Holdcroft, L. Thomas. *The Holy Spirit: A Pentecostal Interpretation.* Revised edition. Abbotsford, BC: CeeTeC Publishing, 1962.

Horton, Harold. *The Gifts of the Spirit.* Springfield, MO: Gospel Publishing House, 1934.

Lim, David. *Spiritual Gifts: A Fresh Look.* Springfield, MO: Gospel Publishing House, 1991.

Palma, Anthony. *The Holy Spirit: A Pentecostal Perspective.* Springfield, MO: Gospel Publishing House, 2001.

Pickett, Fuchsia. *Cultivating the Gifts and Fruit of the Holy Spirit.* Lake Mary, FL: Charisma House, 2004.

Sumrall, Lester. *The Gifts and Ministries of the Holy Spirit.* New Kensington, PA: Whitaker House, 1993.

Underwood, B. E. *Spiritual Gifts, Ministries and Manifestations.* Franklin Springs, GA: Advocate Press, 1984.